Conducting Interinstitutional Comparisons

Paul T. Brinkman, *Editor*
National Center for Higher Education Management Systems

NEW DIRECTIONS FOR INSTITUTIONAL RESEARCH

PATRICK T. TERENZINI, *Editor-in-Chief*
University of Georgia

MARVIN W. PETERSON, *Associate Editor*
University of Michigan

Number 53, Spring 1987

Paperback sourcebooks in
The Jossey-Bass Higher Education Series

Jossey-Bass Inc., Publishers
San Francisco • London

Paul T. Brinkman (ed.).
Conducting Interinstitutional Comparisons.
New Directions for Institutional Research, no. 53.
Volume XIV, Number 1.
San Francisco: Jossey-Bass, 1987.

New Directions for Institutional Research
Patrick T. Terenzini, *Editor-in-Chief*
Marvin W. Peterson, *Associate Editor*

New Directions for Institutional Research is published quarterly by
Jossey-Bass Inc., Publishers (publication number USPS 098-830), and is
sponsored by the Association for Institutional Research. The volume
and issue numbers above are included for the convenience of libraries.
Second-class postage paid at San Francisco, California, and at
additional mailing offices. POSTMASTER: Send address changes to
Jossey-Bass Inc., Publishers, 433 California Street, San Francisco,
California 94104.

Editorial correspondence should be sent to the Editor-in-Chief,
Patrick T. Terenzini, Institute of Higher Education, University of
Georgia, Athens, Georgia 30602.

Library of Congress Catalog Card Number LC 85-645339

International Standard Serial Number ISSN 0271-0579

International Standard Book Number ISBN 1-55542-964-5

Cover art by WILLI BAUM

Manufactured in the United States of America

Ordering Information

The paperback sourcebooks listed below are published quarterly and can be ordered either by subscription or single copy.

Subscriptions cost $40.00 per year for institutions, agencies, and libraries. Individuals can subscribe at the special rate of $30.00 per year *if payment is by personal check.* (Note that the full rate of $40.00 applies if payment is by institutional check, even if the subscription is designated for an individual.) Standing orders are accepted.

Single copies are available at $9.95 when payment accompanies order. (California, New Jersey, New York, and Washington, D.C., residents please include appropriate sales tax.) For billed orders, cost per copy is $9.95 plus postage and handling.

Substantial discounts are offered to organizations and individuals wishing to purchase bulk quantities of Jossey-Bass sourcebooks. Please inquire.

Please note that these prices are for the academic year 1986–1987 and are subject to change without notice. Also, some titles may be out of print and therefore not available for sale.

To ensure correct and prompt delivery, all orders must give either the *name of an individual* or an *official purchase order number.* Please submit your order as follows:

    Subscriptions: specify series and year subscription is to begin.
    Single Copies: specify sourcebook code (such as, IR1) and first two words of title.

Mail orders for United States and Possessions, Latin America, Canada, Japan, Australia, and New Zealand to:
    Jossey-Bass Inc., Publishers
    433 California Street
    San Francisco, California 94104

Mail orders for all other parts of the world to:
    Jossey-Bass Limited
    28 Banner Street
    London EC1Y 8QE

New Directions for Institutional Research Series
Patrick T. Terenzini *Editor-in-Chief*
Marvin W. Peterson, *Associate Editor*

For information about the Association for Institutional Research, write:

AIR Executive Office
314 Stone Building
Florida State University
Tallahassee, FL 32306

(904) 644-4470

Contents

Editor's Notes

Many administrators and analysts believe that comparisons among institutions can be a useful management tool. Others view such comparisons as at best a necessary evil fraught with problems. In any case, interest in interinstitutional comparisons is high. The number of primary and secondary sources of comparative data continues to increase, many institutions and state agencies are developing comparison groups, and the variety of applications of comparative analysis continues to grow.

The purpose of this sourcebook is to provide a comprehensive review of interinstitutional comparisons in higher education. These comparisons are often complex and risky, yet few higher education analysts, let alone administrators, receive formal training in how to conduct such comparisons. This sourcebook seeks to address this situation, and the chapters that follow are designed to introduce readers to the context of comparisons among institutions and to practical strategies for working effectively with interinstitutional data.

This book is aimed primarily at analysts in colleges and universities: institutional researchers, planners, and assistants to deans and other administrators. In addition, the primary audience includes analysts and officers on the staffs of state coordinating or governing boards. Most members of these organizations perform comparative analysis or at least work with comparative data. Institutional administrators also will find this book useful in understanding what characterizes a good comparative study.

When the decision is made to undertake interinstitutional comparisons, one of the first steps in implementation is to determine which institutions to compare. Paul Brinkman and Deborah Teeter address this question in Chapter One. Both have considerable experience in developing techniques for comparative analysis and in working with other analysts to select and use comparison groups. The authors discuss various comparison groups and the options available in developing a peer comparison group and point out that there is more involved than just analysis (for example, the various political dimensions surrounding most comparisons). The chapter illustrates what to watch out for and how to avoid some typical problems.

Selecting a set of institutions for comparison is an important step, and this selection depends on obtaining data on potential comparison institutions. Two chapters are devoted to how to facilitate data acquisition. In Chapter Two Melodie Christal and John Wittstruck describe data that are available from secondary sources. Often the federal government is the source, but the authors, who work with these data regularly, provide a brief overview of other data sources. The chapter is a valuable resource, especially for analysts new to higher education. The data available for comparative analysis are not exhaustive, but knowing where to look can help make the most of current resources.

In Chapter Three John Dunn provides useful suggestions for setting up a formal, ongoing data exchange among institutions. He shares insights gained from his intimate involvement with the establishment of the Higher Education Data System (HEDS). He also discusses some of the other data exchanges that have been established around the nation. Involving an institution in a formal data exchange is a big step and should not be taken without serious thought and planning. This chapter will help analysts chart the right course and prevent future problems and disappointments.

With a list of institutions to compare and data about them, one can embark on a comparative analysis. What is likely to happen? Will alternative comparison groups emerge? Will the questions to be addressed by comparative analysis change? What is likely to be the net effect of the institution's efforts to make use of comparative data? These are the issues addressed by Meredith Whiteley and Frances Stage in Chapter Four. They make a strong case that the use of comparative data will be far more effective if it can be integrated within an institutionwide planning framework. They detail the problems that can arise if such elements as comparative data, peer groups, and so on are introduced without plan into institutional management. The authors also suggest that interinstitutional comparisons need a philosophical or theoretical structure.

Institutional researchers and planners are not the only ones involved in comparative analysis in higher education. Some of the comparisons with the most impact on funding and salaries are performed by individuals who work at the system or the state level. In Chapter Five Marilyn McCoy uses her experience at the system level and in preparing comparative data reports for state-level analysis to delineate the important issues from these perspectives. She discusses how dimensions of interinstitutional analysis vary by type of system and state-level structure. A governing board, for instance, will have different needs for comparative analysis than will a coordinating board with limited powers. The chapter ends with a list of strategies for effective comparative analysis.

In Chapter Six Frederick Lane, James Lawrence, and Herman Mertins present a case study of the use of comparative data to set new funding targets for a major state university. The authors were involved in the analysis as consultants and as institutional participants. Their account of and reflections on the events underscore what all seasoned analysts know: There is more to decision making in universities than just being able to think rationally. The interplay between quantitative analysis and political realities makes this chapter interesting and instructive.

Chapter Seven is a brief review of several of the topics of this source-book and also presents a list of selected articles and books that can provide additional insights on comparative analysis in higher education. Although this book intends to present a comprehensive discussion of interinstitutional comparisons, it is not an exhaustive review of the topic.

Paul T. Brinkman is senior associate at the National Center for Higher Education Management Systems, Boulder, Colorado, where he specializes in comparative data issues and higher education finance.

The analyst can select from a variety of methods for developing institutional comparison groups. Several contextual issues frame the choice of method.

Methods for Selecting Comparison Groups

Paul T. Brinkman, Deborah J. Teeter

The way in which a comparison group is established is crucial to the success or failure of interinstitutional comparisons. Careful planning, which includes choosing among a number of alternative technical procedures, can increase the likelihood that the comparison group will serve its intended purpose.

Why Compare Institutions?

There are many issues for which comparative data are of interest, and these will likely fall under one of the following categories:
- Input-output relationships
- Prices paid
- Prices charged
- Institutional attractiveness
- Institutional structure.

The comparison issue subtly influences the choice of method for determining comparison groups. For example, consider the preferred or required characteristics of the comparative data being sought. Data should be accurate, of course, but how precise and at what level of detail and disaggregation? How can the data be obtained? Are the data sensitive polit-

P. T. Brinkman (ed.). *Conducting Interinstitutional Comparisons.*
New Directions for Institutional Research, no. 53. San Francisco: Jossey-Bass, Spring 1987.

ically? Are the data likely to be ambiguous or misleading? The answers to these questions depend on the comparison issue. In turn, the answers may suggest a particular method of selecting comparison institutions.

Input-Output Relationships. Input-output relationships include the following issues: resource utilization patterns such as class sizes, student-faculty ratios, or proportion of expenditures by function; output patterns such as degrees awarded by field and level, research expenditures per faculty, percent of students graduating or dropping out; relative efficiency measures (or surrogates thereof) such as expenditures per credit hour or per student; and relative effectiveness indicators such as measures of value added or quality rankings. The underlying question is: What do other institutions accomplish with the resources at their disposal?

Prices Paid and Prices Charged. Typically, questions about prices paid focus on faculty salaries or administrator salaries, but they can extend to the prices of other goods and services. The question is: What are other institutions paying to obtain comparable services? Conversely, the question may be: What do other institutions charge for their services? Tuition and fees are the prices that receive the most attention, but room and board charges are also compared.

Institutional Attractiveness. There are many aspects to institutional attractiveness. How successful are other institutions in attracting able students? What proportion of their applicants matriculate? What proportion of their alumnae contribute to the annual fund? How effective are they in obtaining state appropriations? How effective are their faculty in attracting financial support for research projects?

Institutional Structure. Institutional structure comparisons include staff-faculty ratios or administrator-faculty ratios, reporting arrangements, and levels of administration. For many public institutions, a complementary set of questions might focus on how other institutions relate to system offices or to coordinating or system governing boards. Most questions about structure concern varying degrees of regulation and autonomy.

Types of Comparison Groups

When one thinks about interinstitutional comparisons, peer groups most frequently come to mind. However, there are several other types of comparison groups, and all of them can play a legitimate role under certain circumstances. The type needed in a given situation will be important in choosing a method for selecting comparison institutions. The following is an expansion on a comparison group typology developed by Brinkman and Krakower (1983).

Brinkman and Krakower defined four types of comparison groups: competitor, peer, aspiration, and jurisdictional. The first three will be described briefly and then the jurisdictional variety will be discussed as part of a larger set that is labeled *predetermined.*

In the Brinkman and Krakower typology, a competitor group consists of institutions that compete with each other for students or faculty or research dollars, and so on. Institutions that compete in these ways may not be similar in terms of role and scope. The way in which this type of comparison group is used determines the extent to which institutional dissimilarities within the group can be tolerated. For example, consider an institution that assembles a comparison group solely on the basis of competition for faculty for the purpose of comparing faculty salaries. If the "competition" has been established through observation of faculty behavior, interviews with faculty, and so on, this comparison strategy is legitimate with respect to the stated purpose regardless of institutional differences on other dimensions. However, the same comparison group might well be inappropriate if it were to be used for other purposes. For example, any type of comparison that depends on institutional similarity in role and scope will be at risk.

A peer group is comprised of institutions that are similar in role and scope, or mission. In developing peer groups, it is unrealistic to expect to find perfect matches, "clones" as it were, for the home institution. The appropriate goal is a sufficient match on whatever are determined to be the defining characteristics of the home institution. Sufficiency in this context is ultimately a matter of judgment.

To compare means to examine both similarities and differences. The latter are critical for developing an aspiration group that, by definition, includes institutions that are dissimilar to the home institution but are worthy of emulation. When a comparison group contains numerous institutions that are clearly superior to the home institution, the group reflects aspiration more than commonality of mission.

Aspiration groups often masquerade as peer groups. The masquerade may be intentional or unintentional on the part of those developing the comparison group. Typically, individuals outside the institution can see through an unintentional aspiration group easier than those inside, reflecting perhaps some basic psychological phenomena about how individuals see themselves relative to how others see them. In any event, an aspiration group that is presented as if it were a peer group is likely to be costly in the political arena outside the campus. It will put at risk the credibility of almost any comparative data the home institution wishes to use.

Predetermined institutional comparison groups are of four types: natural, traditional, jurisdictional, and classification based. Natural groups are those that are based on one or more of the following: membership in an athletic conference, membership in a regional compact (for instance, the Southern Regional Education Board), location in a region of the country, membership in an association such as the Association of American Universities, or belonging to a consortium such as the Associated Colleges of the Midwest. Most institutions belong to one or more such groups because they have something important in common with others in the group. Natural groups of this kind may form the basis of valid comparisons, but not necessarily. The specific nature of the comparison will always be the final test.

A traditional comparison group is one that has been used for a long time and whose only rationale is just that it has been around for a long time. Like an old coat, it may feel comfortable but it may be out of style and may never have been truly appropriate.

A jurisdictional group consists of institutions that are compared because they are a part of the same political or legal jurisdiction. The basic jurisdiction in this context is the state. The rationale is obvious. The states have responsibility (in varying degrees) for the institutions within their boundaries, especially those in the public domain. It is only natural that elected officials and state agency staff would want to make jurisdictional comparisons, even if the institutions being compared have little else in common. The reasonableness of a particular jurisdictional comparison cannot be determined a priori. Again, the comparison issue is (or should be) the deciding factor.

Institutional classifications designed for national reporting provide another basis for institutional comparisons. The federal government's Center for Education Statistics (formerly known as the National Center for Education Statistics) recently revised its classification, the origins of which go back many decades. The American Association of University Professors uses institutional classifications for reporting comparative faculty salaries. A version of a classification developed at the National Center for Higher Education Management Systems (NCHEMS) is used extensively in *Higher Education Financing in the Fifty States* (McCoy and Halstead, 1984), a major document devoted to comparative analysis. Perhaps the best known is the classification developed by the Carnegie Commission in the 1970s (Carnegie Commission on Higher Education, 1976), which is currently being updated. The rationale for using these classifications for interinstitutional comparisons is twofold: In each instance considerable time and effort have already been spent in grouping similar institutions, and the classifications have established credibility—always an important consideration for any proposed comparison group. The problem in using these ready-made groups, such as public research universities, is that they may still contain too much within-group variation for certain types of comparative analysis.

The advantage of predetermined comparison groups is that the institutions involved frequently have either formally or informally shared data or cooperated with one another in some fashion. As such, using these groups can be attractive to lay persons or to other constituencies of the institution. However, these groups should not be used without a careful assessment of their appropriateness for a given comparison problem. It should never be assumed that this type of group is a reasonable choice.

This discussion of the various types of comparison groups suggests that an institution will likely need more than one comparison group. This is true, but unfortunate. It is costly to develop, use, and maintain more than one comparison group, and using more than one group may cause problems in the political arena. If comparative data are used in advocacy roles to bolster an institution's position, shifting from one comparison group to the next may be viewed with suspicion even though such a move may be conceptually sound.

Politics of Using Comparative Data

Requests for comparative data are never made in a vacuum. It is important not to assume that the preparation of comparative data and the selection of an institutional comparison group are merely an analytical exercise. An assessment of explicit and implicit agendas is called for, as is an assessment of how the intended audience regards comparative data. Organizational and political realities must be considered and a strategy developed accordingly lest the comparative exercise misfire. The salient aspects of those realities are now considered.

Although the requestor's formal agenda is important in that it is reflected directly in the comparison issue and the type of comparison group required, it may be useful to consider informal or hidden agendas. For instance, a formal comparison issue could be focused entirely on faculty salaries, but at a later date the requestor might intend to use the comparison group to examine administrator salaries, level of appropriations, or some other issue. Understanding the full agenda allows one to determine which individuals and constituencies are likely to care about the comparison group and who ought to be involved in its development.

When the requestor and the intended audience agree on the appropriateness of using comparative data in a given situation, the method for selecting comparison institutions probably will not be much of an issue. Agreement about use is likely to result in shared understanding about the type of institutions to be included in the comparison group. By contrast, when agreement is lacking and the intended audience is skeptical, the requestor will find it necessary not only to convince the audience of the merit of using comparative data but also to demonstrate that the method used to select comparison institutions is appropriate.

If the audience is likely to be hostile to the idea of using comparative data, its direct involvement in the process of selecting comparison institutions might mitigate some of the concern, particularly if that concern centers on the validity of the comparison group. When involving individuals from the audience, consider how many to include, when to bring them in, and desirable qualifications, such as influence on colleagues and willingness to participate open-mindedly in the process.

A key to the successful use of comparative data is to properly size up the environment in which the data are to be used and then take the steps necessary to ensure that the audience will be receptive. Failure to lay the proper groundwork may cause extensive delay in the use of comparative data or prohibit its use altogether.

Resources and Other Constraints

The selection of comparison groups can consume considerable resources. An institution must determine how much it is willing to spend in terms of personnel, funds, and computer resources. The type of comparison group, the ability to use existing methodologies, and the receptivity of the audience to comparative data will affect what resources will be necessary for the selection process. Some audiences may require an independent validation of the comparison group by a neutral party; the extent of initial and validation efforts will impact the costs.

Data needed for comparisons often will be readily available in secondary sources (many of them are listed in the next chapter). For some data, however, or for data that must be more timely than that available in secondary sources, the only option is to go directly to the comparison institutions. (Formal data-sharing arrangements are the subject of a later chapter.) For occasional requests of data from other institutions, keep in mind that data that are of mutual interest are more easily obtained than those that serve only the requestor. Reasons for an institution to share data may include the following: (1) The institution requesting assistance might be able to return the favor in the future, (2) it might be desirable to be compared with the institution requesting the data, (3) the results of the data may be desirable, (4) it is a professional courtesy to assist a sister institution, and (5) it may be politically expedient to cooperate (Teeter, 1983).

Time is a valuable commodity as well as a constraint. The time frame for choosing a comparison group may dictate the use of readily available methods, even if they are not fully appropriate. Time constraints may also limit the data (how much, what kind) that can be considered in the selection process. Once a comparison group has been selected, the timeliness of data can also be critical to the success of a comparison. For example, if comparative salary data are to provide a basis for salary allocations, the data must be available within the time frame dictated by the budget cycle.

Developing a Comparison Group

When the comparison issue, the type of comparison group, the audience, the available resources, and the constraints have been analyzed thoroughly, it is time to consider methods for selecting the institutions (presuming that the type of group needed is not of the predetermined variety). Among the other three types of groups, most attention has been directed to peer groups rather than competitor or aspiration groups. Accordingly, selecting peer institutions is the focus here.

A modest typology of approaches to developing institutional peer groups is presented in Figure 1. The top half of the figure describes a continuum of options from a judgment-free (statistical) approach to one that depends entirely on judgment. Both of these approaches can be thought of as ideal types, that is, as convenient fictions serving as logical extremes. The pure statistical approach represents the dream of a completely objective procedure, utterly dependent on data, with no need for judgment. At the other end, judgment (informed opinion) reigns supreme with no need for data or statistical manipulation, at least not in any formal or systematic sense. Between these extremes are the gradations that represent conceptually the kind of procedures that actually are undertaken. The techniques themselves are shown in the bottom half of Figure 1. Each of the techniques will be described briefly in terms of the continuum. Then their inner workings will be examined in more detail.

Cluster analysis and supporting factor analytic and discriminant techniques are characterized by heavy reliance on multivariate statistics and computer processing to manipulate large numbers of institutional descriptors. These techniques tend to deemphasize judgment in the form of practitioner (administrator or faculty) input; however, the analyst using these techniques must make substantive judgments. The hybrid approach incorporates a strong emphasis on data and on input from practitioners, combined with statistical algorithms for manipulating data. The threshold approach also emphasizes a formal, systematic appeal to data and to practitioner input, but it depends little, if at all, on statistical algorithms. Practitioner input is heavily emphasized in the panel approach; some data may be included formally but not systematically or comprehensively.

Cluster Analysis and Related Statistical Procedures. Cluster analysis is the name for a set of statistical procedures designed to help identify

Figure 1. A Typology of Procedures for Developing Peer Groups

Emphasis			
Data plus Statistics	Data plus Statistics plus Judgment	Data plus Judgment	Judgment
Cluster Analysis	Hybrid Approach	Threshold Approach	Panel Review
Technique			

groups of entities that have similar attributes. There are alternative clustering algorithms (see Hartigan, 1975), but all ensure that the entities in a given cluster will be more like one another, with regard to the attributes or variables being evaluated, than the entities in any other cluster. The calculation of statistical distance is central to this procedure, and alternative ways of making the calculation distinguish alternative clustering algorithms.

Cluster analysis, which was developed specifically as a tool for comparative analysis (particularly in biology), seems to be made to order for the peer group selection problem. Clustering routines can be employed with continuous as well as discrete data. An important advantage of the technique is that it does not require the analyst to make arbitrary judgments about the appropriate threshold levels or cut-off points for interval variables included in the analysis. For instance, consider a size criterion that uses an enrollment range of 1,500 to 2,500 students as the matching interval for a home institution with 2,000 students. If an institution with 2,500 students is an acceptable match, how can one reasonably exclude an institution with 2,510 students? This type of problem plagues virtually any threshold analysis, but clustering avoids it. In the example, the institution with 2,510 students would simply be assigned a slightly larger statistical distance.

Cluster analysis has its drawbacks. First, it does not provide definitive solutions. Judgment is still needed to decide both how and where group boundaries will be drawn. Sometimes the clustering routine will reveal clear-cut, "natural" boundaries but usually not for the entire sample being studied. Second, judgment is required in choosing weights to assign to variables entering the analysis. This requirement is not avoided by assigning equal weights to all variables (the typical default option). Third, the way data are standardized in cluster analysis can cause problems. Variables that have the largest variance will have the largest impact on the cluster results, irrespective of whether that makes sense substantively.

Factor analysis is a means of conveniently incorporating a large amount of data in the peer selection process. It is sometimes used in this capacity as a preliminary step before undertaking cluster analysis. Factor analysis will be effective as long as some of the original descriptors are a measure of the same attribute or concept. For instance, total enrollment, total number of degrees awarded, and total expenditures for instruction are descriptors whose values are likely to be highly correlated. They will generate a factor that the statistical technique will isolate and that the analyst subsequently will no doubt interpret as size. Each institution in the analysis can then be given a factor score that locates it on the size dimension. This score can replace the original three descriptors, thus reducing the data set, and the one score can be used for a subsequent cluster analysis.

Factor analysis can be used to generate groups of similar institutions directly by using what is called Q-factor analysis (see Stephenson, 1953). Standard forms of factor analysis can be combined with multidimensional scaling to create peer groups. Discussions of the latter approach can be found in Cole and Cole (1970) and in Smart, Elton, and Martin (1980). However, higher education peer groups are more commonly developed using factor analysis in combination with cluster analysis; examples include Elsass and Lingenfelter (1980), and Terenzini, Hartmark, Lorang, and Shirley (1980).

Factor analysis, while suitable for these purposes, has its drawbacks. The reliability of its results are directly related to sample size. Comrey (1973) believes that analyses based on samples of fewer than three hundred cases have only fair reliability. The variables used in the analysis are supposed to be normally distributed, which can be a difficult assumption to meet for some institutional descriptors. Judgment is required in selecting the type of rotation to use (essentially, how to position the factor axes relative to the data vectors; for an excellent conceptual discussion, see Gould, 1981). There is no right answer, mathematically speaking. Judgment is also used in determining the number of factors to extract to create factor scores; again, there is no right answer from the standpoint of the mathematics involved. Both choices will make a difference in the final result. As in cluster analysis, data standardization can influence the factor results in undesirable ways.

Apart from these statistical matters, it should be noted that the abstractness of factor scores can cause problems for the lay person. For instance, an institution with no Ph.D. programs will nonetheless be assigned a score on the Ph.D. dimension should that be a factor in the chosen solution. Experience shows that lay persons may have difficulty in understanding that score, perhaps because they see the variable in discrete, either/or terms. More generally, the nonstatistician will simply have to take on faith that the factor-clustering approach is appropriate for establishing a particular peer group and that the various human interventions required by these procedures have been reasonable.

To examine statistically the results of the clustering techniques, one can use discriminant analysis. This technique provides a way of assessing both the goodness of fit between institutions and their assigned groups and the relative statistical influence of variables employed in the cluster analysis. Discriminant analysis is used in this manner in the previously mentioned studies by Elsass and Lingenfelter (1980) and Terenzini, Hartmark, Lorang, and Shirley (1980). (Discussion of this procedure can be found in most texts on multivariate statistics.)

Cluster analysis and the supportive statistical techniques should be considered seriously by a researcher confronted with the task of mapping the universe of institutions (or a large portion of it). It is less clear that the approach makes sense when the task is simply to find a peer group for a particular institution. Analysts in state agencies with many institutions for which to find peers fall somewhere in the middle on this evaluative continuum; available resources and political considerations will probably be decisive.

Hybrid Approaches. Various hybrid approaches to forming peer groups are conceivable. One such approach is presented here. It is used by the Kansas Board of Regents to identify peer groups for the six four-year institutions under its jurisdiction. (A complete description can be found in Cleaver, 1981.) There are ten distinct steps in the overall process.

1. A subset of states from which peer institutions can be drawn is selected based on criteria such as population, urban/rural mix, and industrialization.

2. Nominal variables are used to create a subset of institutions that ultimately will be rank ordered in terms of similarity to each of the Regents' institutions. To be in that subset, an institution must be public, four year, and not a branch campus.

3. The subset of all candidate institutions is divided into three groups based on the number of Ph.D. programs offered and the size of the city in which the candidate is located, to correspond with a three-part division of the six Kansas institutions.

4. Campus officials review the institutions in each of the groups and discard any institutions whose curriculum is excessively narrow (one with almost all its degrees in engineering or medicine). Any institution that remains in one of the groups is judged to be a viable candidate to be included in the final list of peers.

5. The next task is to arrange the remaining institutions in the order of their similarity with the respective Kansas institution. This involves selecting and assembling detailed information on institutional enrollments (full-time equivalents [FTE], head count, percent at graduate level), finances (percentage distribution of educational and general expenditures by instruction, research, public service, all other expenditures, and restricted), and degrees awarded (the twenty-four categories of the old HEGIS two-digit program classification by four degree levels).

6. The first of a series of statistical algorithms is introduced as the raw data values for the variables assembled in step five are normalized by conversion to z-scores.

7. Comparison scores are created by calculating the difference between each candidate institution's z-scores and its respective Kansas institution.

8. These comparison scores are then standardized.

9. Weights are applied to the comparison scores (the Kansas team gave degrees awarded the highest weight, finances the lowest).

10. The standardized and weighted comparison scores are summed to produce a similarity score. The candidate institutions are then rank

ordered on these similarity scores, which concludes the statistical portion of the process.

The rank-ordered listings can be used in various ways to support interinstitutional comparisons, as will be shown in the illustration below.

Threshold Approach. Thresholds, or cut-off points, are used in both cluster analysis and hybrid approaches, but only secondarily. It is possible to rely primarily on thresholds and raw data.

For several years, NCHEMS has been assisting individual institutions and state agencies in developing institutional peer groups. The procedure used combines raw data, thresholds, weights, and a very modest statistical algorithm. It is not a pure threshold approach, but it comes close in practice, beginning with the selection of comparison dimensions. A standard form, containing a set of nominal variables and a set of interval variables, is provided to the home institution. The form serves as a guideline and can be customized as desired. The nominal institutional descriptors include control (public or private), land-grant status (yes or no), first professional medical programs (yes or no), and location (urban or rural and geographic region). The home institution decides which of these characteristics are important in selecting peers, and their decisions are incorporated in a first pass through the Higher Education General Information Survey (HEGIS) universe of institutions. Any institution not matching on an important dimension is eliminated from further consideration.

Depending on the type of institution involved and the criteria established, this first step can significantly reduce the list of candidate institutions. For instance, if the candidates must be land-grant institutions, the size of the relevant universe is reduced from 3,300 or so to 72. A location criterion stating that the candidate institutions must be located in a particular region can have a similar or even more drastic effect.

It is useful to think of a threshold approach as a procedure for reducing the universe until a residue of acceptable institutions is all that remains. Institutions are eliminated because they are too different from the home institution on at least one important dimension. The comparison issue should be used to determine which differences cannot be tolerated.

Nominal variables alone seldom result in an acceptable peer group. In the NCHEMS approach, the next step for the home institution is to establish additional criteria using a set of interval variables. Three decisions must be made: which descriptors are relevant, how important is each relevant descriptor, and what is the acceptable range of values for each relevant descriptor. For instance, size might be deemed relevant and very important. If the number of FTE students is chosen as the measure of size and if the home institution has 17,000 FTE students, the acceptable range might be set at 12,000 to 30,000. Other descriptors reflecting the level of separately budgeted research, degree-level emphasis, curricular emphasis, and additional aspects of enrollment can be operationalized in a similar fashion.

After the interval variables have been determined, a second computer pass is made through the remaining candidate institutions. The institutions are assigned points based on the number of times they miss a range and the level of importance assigned to each of the missed ranges. This simple algorithm yields a rank-ordered list of candidate institutions in terms of their closeness to the home institution. Individuals at the home institution then examine the list and make a final selection of peers from it.

That last step is an appeal to expert judgment. In rank ordering institutions, the NCHEMS algorithm ignores the extent to which an institution is within or outside of a particular interval variable range. For example, using the lower bound on enrollment of 12,000 students, an institution with 11,990 would be penalized fully for missing the range, while one with 12,010 would be treated as a good match, ceteris paribus. As noted earlier, this is the basic weakness of the threshold approach, for it is difficult to imagine how such a minute difference in enrollment between two candidate institutions could possibly have any real significance. There is also the possibility that a given candidate institution might miss on only one range and thus be ranked high even though the extent of that miss was enormous. Thus, for this particular threshold approach to work, it is crucial that individuals at the home institution examine the rank-ordered list—and accompanying data array—and take appropriate action. The home institution might elect to include or exclude the two institutions with nearly identical enrollments (at least relative to that variable), while deciding that a particular wide miss renders a candidate institution unacceptable for further consideration.

Panel Approach. The term *panel approach* refers to the development of a peer group primarily through informed judgment. No statistical algorithms are used, and data are used only informally; consensus among knowledgeable individuals is the basis for the selection of peers. Descriptions of this approach are difficult to find because of its simplicity. Nonetheless, peer groups developed in this manner are probably more the rule than the exception, although experience suggests that the procedure may sometimes be replaced, or at least validated, by more systematic, data-based approaches, especially when peer comparisons play an important part in funding or allocation decisions. A limitation on its replacement is the lack of widely acceptable quantitative measures of qualitative dimensions.

Comparison Dimensions. An important, early step in each of the above procedures except the panel approach is the selection of the comparison dimensions, or institutional characteristics, that are to be used for deciding which institutions to include in the peer group. Several general rules for selecting comparison dimensions follow:

1. Involve the key participants at this early stage. Comparison dimensions operate somewhat as a first premise. Individuals will have a

difficult time challenging the composition of a peer group that is based on criteria they themselves have chosen.

2. Use the fewest possible dimensions needed for the task. Information is seldom a free good, and an overabundance of data can actually reduce information content. A proposed comparison dimension should be clearly relevant to the comparison issue.

3. To avoid circular arguments, use criteria that operationalize institutional mission or characterize important aspects of the environment within which institutions must operate. Do not use criteria that measure some aspect of resource allocation or utilization. The latter often are the characteristics being evaluated.

4. Start with concepts, and then go to measures. For example, is institutional size worth including among the criteria? If so, then how shall it be measured?

5. The best measures usually are those that focus on mission and stay away from resources. For example, the number of students enrolled would often be a better choice as a measure of size than total expenditures. Ultimately, of course, the choice should make sense relative to the comparison issue. In some cases, more than one measure of a particular concept or comparison dimension may be appropriate.

An Illustration

Do these different methods lead to results that are significantly different? This question is virtually impossible to answer in universal terms, but the following example is an illustration of the kind and degree of differentiation that can occur.

The home institution is the University of Kansas (KU), a large state university not a land-grant institution, that places a high emphasis on graduate education at both the master's and doctoral levels, has a moderate amount of research for an institution of its kind, a broad curriculum with two-thirds of its degrees awarded in professional areas (education, business, communications, and so on), a law school, and a medical school located on another campus.

Table 1 displays peer institutions for KU based on alternative selection techniques. The list based on cluster analysis (of factor scores) was taken from a study by the Illinois Board of Higher Education (1985). It is designed to support an analysis of average faculty salaries. The second list, based on the Kansas Board of Regents hybrid approach, was provided by the Office of Institutional Research at KU. A subset of the list is used for general purpose peer group comparisons including detailed financial and faculty salary comparisons. The third list, based on a threshold approach, was provided by NCHEMS and was meant to be used for faculty salary comparisons. The fourth list, based on a panel approach, was also provided by KU. It is used for detailed financial comparisons; the hybrid

Table 1. Peer Institutions for the University of Kansas
Based on Alternative Selection Techniques

Illinois Cluster	Kansas Hybrid	NCHEMS Threshold	Kansas Panel
Brigham Young	Connecticut	Cincinnati	Colorado
Cincinnati	South Carolina	Colorado	Iowa
Colorado	Colorado	Oklahoma	Oklahoma
Connecticut	Houston	Iowa	Oregon
Indiana	Arizona	Oregon	North Carolina
Iowa	Wayne State	Florida State	
Minnesota	Oregon	South Carolina	
Ohio State	New Mexico	Utah	
Penn State	Cincinnati	New Mexico	
Pittsburgh	Kentucky	Indiana	
Purdue	West Virginia	Virginia	
Rutgers	Tennessee		
SUNY Buffalo	Missouri		
SUNY Stony Brook	Oklahoma		
Syracuse	Iowa		
Virginia	Georgia		

approach was developed to objectively verify the panel institutions as appropriate peers. Each of the first three lists were developed using data from 1981–1982.

The differences among the listings are not dramatic, given the range of institutions in the overall population, but neither are they insignificant. The cluster-based list includes two private institutions (a result of a policy decision rather than of anything inherent in the clustering routine), five land-grant institutions (Minnesota, Ohio State, Purdue, Penn State, and Rutgers), two institutions from each of three states and three institutions from one state, and several of the largest and most comprehensive institutions (Minnesota, Ohio State, and Penn State). From purely a Kansas salary comparison standpoint, one could argue that only the heavy dependence on Great Lakes states and New York is objectionable. If this list were to be used for other purposes, the presence of land-grant institutions, very large and comprehensive institutions, and private institutions might all be cause for concern.

The inclusion of several urban institutions (Cincinnati, Houston, and Wayne State) in the hybrid-based list might be of concern with respect to salary comparisons, although the urban areas in question are not at the top of the cost-of-living scale. The five land-grant institutions (Connecticut, Arizona, West Virginia, Tennessee, and Missouri) could be a problem if something other than salaries were the comparison issue. The hybrid list displays the sixteen institutions with the smallest statistical distance from KU (sixteen were selected for Table 1 to match the number of institutions in the cluster list). It should be noted that the peer group used in Kansas for KU consists of five institutions (from the panel approach), which were selected from among the top thirty-seven on the hybrid list. As mentioned earlier, the hybrid approach was used to validate the peer group established by the panel approach.

Table 2 shows values for the key variables that guided the selection of the threshold-based list. The list includes only a single urban institution (Cincinnati), no land-grant institutions, a broad geographical spread, and a fairly tight congruence on the interval variables. All the institutions have law schools, and they all have substantive offerings in business or engineering. These curricular areas, as well as the extent and proportion of separately budgeted research, have implications for faculty salaries. Some of the institutions have medical schools. This is not important for faculty salary comparisons because of the way in which salaries for medical staff are reported nationally. It certainly could be important if some other comparison issue were considered, such as state appropriations per student.

The panel-based list contains one institution, the University of North Carolina at Chapel Hill (UNC), that does not appear on the other lists. In the cluster analysis it is grouped with institutions such as the University of California at Berkeley, the University of Michigan, and others of the most highly rated public and large private institutions (not shown). In the hybrid analysis, it ranks thirty-seventh in statistical distance from KU, the furthest of any institution included in the panel-based list. UNC did much better in the threshold-based listing. It placed fifth in the rank ordering, missing the ranges on only three of twenty-one descriptors. The analyst eliminated it from the final list, however, because the difference in the amount of sponsored research was deemed to be too large to tolerate ($57 million at UNC compared to $18 million at KU, in 1981–1982). The inclusion of UNC in the panel-based list has an aspirational overtone, which would not be surprising for that sort of approach. The official rationale in Kansas for continuing to include UNC as a peer despite the results of their hybrid analysis is twofold: (1) For comparisons of activities funded through state funds and tuition, UNC is a reasonable peer for KU, and (2) system considerations enhance the acceptability of UNC. North Carolina State is a good match for Kansas State and with UNC included in the KU group, the two largest Kansas institutions can draw their peers from the same five states.

Two points were meant to be reinforced in this illustration. One, there will be some candidate institutions in a list of potential peers that are not clearly either acceptable or unacceptable. Therefore, it is important to get some measure of agreement about priorities before serious data analysis begins (before conceptual vision is overwhelmed by the concreteness of numerical measurements). Two, any technical approach remains rooted in a larger organizational and political context.

Table 2. Selected Comparison Dimensions Used to Create Threshold-Based List of Peers for the University of Kansas

Institution	Number of FTE Students	Percent of Doctoral Degrees	Percent of Engineering and Business Degrees	Expenditures for Research (millions of dollars)	Expenditure Ratio: Research/Instruction
University of Kansas	20,364	5.5	25	18	0.37
University of Cincinnati	23,138	3.5	33	24	0.27
University of Colorado, Boulder	20,663	4.9	28	28	0.53
University of Oklahoma	18,971	3.5	32	15	0.34
University of Iowa	24,717	6.4	24	35	0.37
University of Oregon	13,974	5.9	16	10	0.26
Florida State University	19,013	6.0	21	18	0.32
University of South Carolina	19,567	2.8	26	13	0.23
University of Utah	19,937	4.9	27	35	0.56
University of New Mexico	17,540	3.8	19	12	0.30
Indiana University	29,161	6.3	29	19	0.22
University of Virginia	16,055	4.5	20	29	0.47
Mean	20,258	4.8	25	21	0.35
Standard Deviation	3,829	1.2	4.9	8	0.11
University of Kansas/Mean	1.01	1.14	1.00	0.84	1.05

Aspiration and Competitor Groups

Developing an aspiration group is only slightly different than developing a peer group because the matching process in both cases is focused on institutional mission. The difference is that the home institution adjusts its sights upward and selects comparison institutions that share its mission generally but are more successful in achieving it. For example, a small private institution of modest accomplishments might aspire to become one of the best small private institutions. A large, but undistinguished, public university might aspire to be counted among the distinguished large public institutions—or at least to be funded as if it were!

The panel and threshold approaches are the easiest to use when developing an aspiration group. In many instances, superiority is at least partly subjective, so the informed experts on the panel are in their element when asked to select institutions worth emulating. In the threshold-based approach described above, one need only shift the ranges of the important interval variables in the desired direction and proceed as before. For instance, a fledgling research university might set the midpoint of the matching range for sponsored research expenditures at three times its current level, the proportion of doctoral degrees at twice its current proportion, and so on. This procedure has an inherent, useful concreteness to it because the target is specified in quantitative terms as opposed to more abstract goal formulations.

Developing competitor groups requires a very different strategy. The data required will depend on what the competition is for—students, faculty, research dollars, and so on. If the competition is for students, then data on student choices and the distribution of student types among the institutions in a geographic region will be needed. Similarly, when competing for faculty, data are needed on the movement of faculty from graduate schools to initial positions, and from one position to another. For larger institutions especially, competition for faculty tends to be as much by discipline as by institution, which suggests that department chairpersons are a major source of relevant data. Gathering data on the competition dimensions serves to identify the competition.

Updating

After comparison institutions are identified, periodic reevaluations of the composition of the group may be required, depending on the purpose of the comparison and the type of comparison group. Given the volatility of higher education funding, institutions selected to benchmark funding needs may require frequent reexamination. Any significant change in the mission of the home institution also would be reason to reexamine an existing peer group. Such changes can take place in a peer

22

institution as well, which suggests the advisability of assembling mission-related data on the institutions in a peer group every three to five years.

After using a peer group for a number of years and assuming that the importance of comparisons justifies the cost, there may be utility in trying an alternative method for selecting peers. Depending on the outcome, this could serve to reinforce earlier decisions about the composition of the peer group or indicate the need for revision. There are also times when it is best to leave things as they are—even if they are not perfect.

Sharing Procedures

Institutions or other organizations that have developed formal procedures for identifying comparison institutions have on occasion made their data and procedures available for a small fee. Since development costs can be high, this is an attractive service either to offer or to use, depending on the circumstances.

References

Brinkman, P., and Krakower, J. *Comparative Data for Administrators in Higher Education.* Boulder, Colo: National Center for Higher Education Management Systems, 1983.

Carnegie Commission on Higher Education. *A Classification of Institutions of Higher Education.* Berkeley, Calif.: Carnegie Commission on Higher Education, 1976.

Cleaver, G. S. "Analysis to Determine a Ranking in Similarity for Institutions in Higher Education." Paper presented at the Annual Conference of the Society for College and University Planning, Omaha, Nebraska, July 12-15, 1981.

Cole, N. A., and Cole, J.W.L. *An Analysis of Spatial Configuration and Its Application to Research in Higher Education.* ACT Research Report, no. 35. Iowa City, Iowa: American College Testing Program, 1970.

Comrey, A. L. *A First Course in Factor Analysis.* New York: Academic Press, 1973.

Elsass, J. E., and Lingenfelter, P. E. *An Identification of College and University Peer Groups.* Springfield: Illinois Board of Education, 1980.

Gould, S. J. *The Mismeasure of Man.* New York: Norton, 1981.

Hartigan, J. A. *Clustering Algorithms.* New York: Wiley, 1975.

Illinois Board of Higher Education. *College and University Comparison Groups.* Springfield: Illinois Board of Higher Education, 1985.

McCoy, M., and Halstead, D. K. *Higher Education Financing in the Fifty States: Interstate Comparisons Fiscal Year 1982.* (2nd ed.) Boulder, Colo.: National Center for Higher Education Management Systems, 1984.

Smart, J. C., Elton, C. F., and Martin, R. O. "Qualitative and Conventional Indices of Benchmark Institutions." Paper presented at the Twentieth Annual Forum of the Association for Institutional Research, Atlanta, Georgia, April 29, 1980.

Stephenson, W. *The Study of Behavior.* Chicago: University of Chicago Press, 1953.

Teeter, D. J. "The Politics of Comparing Data with Other Institutions." In J. W. Firnberg and W. F. Lasher (eds.), *The Politics and Pragmatics of Institutional Research.* New Directions for Institutional Research, no. 38. San Francisco: Jossey-Bass, 1983.

Terenzini, P. T., Hartmark, L., Lorang, W. G., Jr., and Shirley, R. C. "A Conceptual and Methodological Approach to the Identification of Peer Institutions." *Research in Higher Education*, 1980, *12*, 347-364.

Paul T. Brinkman is senior associate at the National Center for Higher Education Management Systems, Boulder, Colorado.

Deborah J. Teeter is director of institutional research, University of Kansas.

A multitude of data sources exist that can be used for institutional comparisons.

Sources of Comparative Data

Melodie E. Christal, John R. Wittstruck

Where does one find and how does one obtain data for institutional comparisons? Although such data may be directly obtained from colleges and universities, comparative data typically are more readily available from secondary or even tertiary sources. This chapter provides information on these secondary and tertiary sources.

Opportunities for Data Collection

The federal data collection effort for a few higher education characteristics began around 1870 and then took a large step forward in 1929 when the U.S. Department of Education first sent surveys to institutions. The next major advance came in the mid-1960s with the Higher Education General Information Surveys (HEGIS) for the National Center for Education Statistics (NCES) (Brinkman and Krakower, 1983). Higher education interests were served well for twenty years by HEGIS, but in the early 1980s it became obvious that additional data were needed if important questions about not just higher but also postsecondary education were to be adequately addressed. Thus, in 1986 the first steps are being taken to implement a replacement for HEGIS (and other federal surveys). This new survey, known as the Integrated Postsecondary Education Data Sys-

P. T. Brinkman (ed.). *Conducting Interinstitutional Comparisons.*
New Directions for Institutional Research, no. 53. San Francisco: Jossey-Bass, Spring 1987.

tems (IPEDS) will be discussed below. Another major contribution to the national data pool, the National Science Foundation Surveys of Higher Education Institutions, began in the 1950s.

The higher education data collection effort at the state level was fueled after World War II by the tremendous growth in the enterprise. Most states now maintain extensive data bases on their public colleges and universities and sometimes on private institutions as well. In most instances, the state data base for higher education will reside in the state higher education agencies, consisting of coordinating boards or governing boards, that have either all or some portion of a state's public institutions within their purview. There are also federal data collection efforts that have a state focus, such as the Commerce Department's *Census of Governments* series, which contain state-level comparative data on higher education. The need for data is equally great during periods of steady state or retrenchment, as in the past during the growth of higher education.

In addition to the federal and state-level data collection efforts, the nation's three regional higher education associations (Southern Regional Education Board, New England Board of Higher Education, and Western Interstate Commission on Higher Education), numerous special interest associations and institutions with cooperative arrangements also participate in interinstitutional data collection endeavors. The number of data sources has increased steadily during the last several decades, and there is every indication that the trend will continue.

IPEDS. One of the tasks charged to the Center for Education Statistics (formerly the National Center for Education Statistics) by Congress is to report on the condition of postsecondary education in the United States. To do this, the Center for Education Statistics must describe postsecondary education and follow changes in its size, character, providers, and participants. In the past NCES accomplished this through three surveys: HEGIS, the Vocational Education Data System (VEDS), and the Survey of Noncollegiate Postsecondary Schools with Occupational Programs. As NCES operated and assessed its institutional survey systems, it became aware of several inherent methodological problems that made a complete description of the postsecondary education enterprise difficult to provide. For example, because of considerable overlap in the data collection universes associated with HEGIS and VEDS, institutions involved in both of these collection efforts were confronted with an unnecessary data burden. More important from the perspective of the ultimate objective, NCES had difficulty synthesizing the data, owing to differences in data definitions, survey procedures, and so on. In addition, several segments of a larger universe of providers of postsecondary education were not included in any of the three surveys.

In recognition of these problems and based on recommendations from the postsecondary education community, NCES developed the Integrated Postsecondary Education Data System. In IPEDS, data elements, data definitions, and procedures have been designed to minimize data burden and duplication at the institutional level and to facilitate statistical summaries that can reach various sectors of postsecondary education. Although a number of changes have been made, the system is not a totally new data collection system; instead, it is built on existing NCES collection efforts and contains links with the old surveys. It is these links that will allow noninterrupted data comparisons between the HEGIS surveys and IPEDS, an important consideration for researchers interested in time-series analysis. IPEDS has been approved by the Office of Management and Budget for three years from 1986 through 1988.

Unit of Analysis. When looking for data sources for data comparisons, the unit of analysis is an important consideration. There are several choices. The most disaggregated choice involves institutional components—programs, departments, colleges within a university, or other budget or activity centers within the institution. Cost analysis at an institution usually includes this type of internal unit level comparison. Less frequently, departments or other activity units will be compared across institutions. Such matters as resource utilization, salaries, and work load are usually the issues in question.

Another unit of analysis is the institutional level, where comparisons are made between or among entire institutions. Examples of institutional analyses include comparisons of faculty salaries, tuition rates, costs per student, and academic programs or services offered.

A third unit of analysis, the state level, is becoming increasingly important. Interstate comparisons of financial support of higher education have become integral factors in the funding process in many states. A fourth possibility, national level comparisons, are worth mentioning for the sake of completeness, but data sources for such comparisons are not included in the discussion that follows.

Potential Problems. When using data for comparative purposes, it is wise to be prepared for some potential problems. One of the most common criticisms of higher education data obtained from secondary and tertiary sources is that the data lack timeliness. Gathering, editing, reporting, and disseminating data is a time-consuming process, and, as a result, the data are often one or two years old at the time of release. This is especially true with national data collections. A survey of state agency staff (Wittstruck, 1985) shows that data are considered timely if they are available one year after the closing date of the survey. (Efforts are being made to make IPEDS data available on a more timely basis than has been the case for most HEGIS data. In particular, the increased use of electronic storage and electronic communications should shorten the turnaround time for IPEDS data.)

The frequency of data collection and changes in the data elements collected can also cause problems, especially when trend analysis is important. Some data collections occur only biennially, or less frequently, or the data elements collected may vary from year to year. For instance, HEGIS enrollment data are collected by major program and racial/ethnic category only in even-numbered years. Inadequate coverage in a data collection is yet another frequent problem. A data base may be limited to one type of institution or fail to include important data elements. An important example of the latter failure is the absence at present of any national, comprehensive source of data on part-time faculty at four-year institutions (fortunately, IPEDS will remedy this problem).

There have been several studies recently on the comparability of HEGIS data among institutions, and most of the results are applicable in general terms to other data sources. The problems with HEGIS data fall into three categories: universe definition, funding differences, and reporting problems (Lapovsky, 1983).

In the HEGIS universe there can be major differences among the institutions and states in terms of the functions that are included for reporting purposes. For example, some medical schools have their own FICE codes and report separately to HEGIS, while other medical schools combine their data and integrate it with broader institutional reports. It is often difficult to determine what entities an institution includes in its data reporting. Differences in this regard can lead to comparative results that are seriously misleading.

A similar problem exists with funding differences. Some institutions may have special programs funded directly, whereas other institutions may have special programs funded from a central agency. Unless a special cost allocation is made, the funds from the agency never appear in the latter institutions' finance reports. Also, different institutions may include different line items or activities in their reporting. For example, in some instances fringe benefits are paid from institutional accounts, and in other cases they are funded through a central state agency. Similarly, intercollegiate athletic revenues and expenditures are sometimes handled by an athletic association that is a separate, nondegree-granting entity, and the data are therefore not reported in HEGIS.

Reporting problems can occur as the result of insufficient or different interpretations of instructions and insufficient incentives to correctly report the data. One example of a potential reporting problem is the definition of the full-time equivalent of part-time students. In the HEGIS enrollment survey, institutions are given three very different options for determining full-time equivalency.

As for the quality of HEGIS data in general, a survey of higher education institutions and state agencies showed that 85 percent of the respondents felt that the accuracy of the data was acceptable or better (Andrew, Fortune, and McCluskey, 1980). Firnberg and Christal (1984) concur with this finding and state that HEGIS is the best complete data set that can be used for comparisons in higher education. They also note, however, that it is desirable to know the reporting practices of the institutions that are used for interinstitutional comparisons so that adjustments can be made as needed.

Data Sources

Comparative analyses can be applied to any number of management concerns, including salaries, tuition rates, work loads, productivity, expenditures, revenues, outcomes, and so on. The most widely used data deal with enrollments, degrees awarded, finances, and faculty salaries.

Most sources consist of data bases that are national in scope and contain data on all institutions in the nation, on a subset of institutions that are located in various parts of the nation, on all the states, and so on. Data sources that are national in scope typically do not deal with the intrainstitutional level of analysis, although there are important exceptions. Although the data source listings are extensive, we acknowledge that some sources may have been inadvertently overlooked. We also remind the reader that state agencies frequently are good secondary sources of data, but they are not included systematically in the listings that follow.

Finance. Sources of financial data are listed in Table 1. Only three of the data sources provide financial data at the institutional level, and only one provides data below that level. Finance data by department or discipline are available at individual institutions, of course, and at many state higher education agencies, such as a coordinating or governing boards.

For institutional-level analysis, the HEGIS "Financial Statistics of Institutions of Higher Education" is the most comprehensive of the sources listed in Table 1. It provides current funds revenues by source (for example, tuition and fees, state appropriations, endowment, and so on), current funds expenditures by function (for example, instruction, research, student services, and so on), physical plant assets and indebtedness, details of endowment assets, and a statement of changes in fund balances. Because the data provided in the survey are so extensive, it can require up to one year (or more) for the Center for Statistics to collect, process, and release the data for public use. This is perhaps the major drawback to this particular data source.

Aspects of the quality of HEGIS data generally have been discussed. HEGIS financial data have come under special scrutiny. For example, they have been evaluated by being compared to audited data that were coded to standards set by the National Association of College and University Business Officers (NACUBO) and the American Institute of Certified Public Accountants (AICPA) (Minter and Conger, 1979a,b,c; Patrick and

Table 1. Finance

TITLE	CONTENT	PUA*	FREQUENCY	SOURCE
Financial Statistics of Institutions of Higher Education for Fiscal Year Ending 19xx	Current funds revenues by source; current funds expenditures by function; physical plant assets and indebtedness; and endowment assets.	I	Annually as part of HEGIS. Will be continued in IPEDS as "Financial Statistics."	Information Office Center for Statistics/OERI U. S. Department of Education 400 Maryland Avenue Washington D. C. 20202 (800) 424-1616
Grapevine	State tax legislation; state appropriations for colleges and universities; and legislation affecting education beyond high school.	IS	Monthly since 1958.	Center for Higher Education 1535 DeGarmo Hall College of Education Illinois State University Normal, IL 61761 (309) 438-7655
Appropriations of State Tax Funds for Operating Expenses of Higher Education	Current fiscal year appropriations for higher education reported by institution. Includes a state summary of current year appropriations, maps illustrating 2-year and 10-year rate changes, and a narrative summary.	IS	Annually since 1959.	NASULGC One Dupont Circle, Suite 710 Washington, D. C. 20036 (202) 293-7070
Financial Support of Higher Education in Washington: A National Comparison	State and local appropriations per FTE; state and local appropriations and student operating fees per FTE; and ratios using enrollment and population data.	SN	Annually.	Washington Higher Education Coordinating Board 908 East Fifth Avenue, EW-11 Olympia, WA 98504 (206) 753-3241
Comparative Financial Statistics for Community and Junior Colleges	Comparative financial and other data on sample of public 2-year colleges; median and quartile scores are provided according to size of institution.	N	Annually since 1977-78.	NACUBO One Dupont Circle, Suite 500 Washington, D. C. 20036 (202) 861-2563
Quarterly Summary of State and Local Tax Revenue: Series GT	For the current quarter and specified periods, national totals for state and local revenue by level of government and type of tax; property tax collection in selected areas; and collection of selected state taxes by state.	SN	Quarterly.	Data User Services Division Customer Service Bureau of Census Washington, D. C. 20036 (301) 763-4100
Tax Capacity of the Fifty States	Estimates of the tax capacity for each state using a representative tax system. Data are also provided by type of tax for each state.	SN	Annually.	Advisory Commission on Intergovernmental Relations Washington, D. C. 20575 (202) 653-5540

Table 1. *(continued)*

How States Compare in Financing Higher Education	Current fiscal year appropriations and supporting data including population, high school graduates, enrollment, and taxes for public institutions.	S	Annually since 1978.	Kent Halstead Office of Educational Research and Improvement 1200 19th Street N. W. Washington, D. C. 20208 (202) 254-5928
Survey of Scientific and Engineering Expenditures at Universities and Colleges	Information from 500-600 institutions on academic spending for scientific and engineering activities.	DI	Originated in 1954; annually since 1972.	NSF Division of Science Resources Studies 1800 G Street, N. W. Washington, D. C. 20550 (202) 634-4673
Voluntary Support of Education	The number of contributors and amounts of gifts to higher education are given according to the type of source.	I	Annually since 1954-55.	Council for Financial Aid to Education 680 Fifth Avenue New York, NY 10019
Federal Support to Universities, Colleges, and Selected Nonprofit Institutions	Federal support for scientific research and development is provided.	ISN	Annually.	Superintendent of Documents U. S. Government Printing Office Washington, D. C. 20550

*Primary Unit of Analysis: D=Department or Discipline
I=Institution
S=State
N=National

Collier, 1979). There were two major findings. The first was that there was considerable discrepancy between HEGIS financial data and data coded to AICPA–NACUBO standards. For example, for fiscal year 1977 about 20 percent of the 125 private institutions studied either overreported or underreported instructional expenditures by 15 percent or more. The figures were worse for academic support but somewhat better on the whole for data on revenues by source. The investigators concluded that disaggregated HEGIS financial data should be used with extreme caution. The second major finding was that HEGIS financial data in the aggregate compared very favorably with the audited and coded data.

A financial statistic that will be of much interest to public institutions as well as to state higher education agencies is the appropriation of state dollars to higher education. Although included in HEGIS, both the "Grapevine" and "Appropriations of State Tax Funds for Operating Expenses of Higher Education" are more timely sources for this data for both individual institutions and state aggregations.

Staff and Personnel. Staff and personnel data sources are listed in Table 2. The data in this area tend to be primarily salary data at the national level and, in many cases, only for faculty members. Administrators and support staff in higher education institutions are largely overlooked, at least in terms of being connected to a specific institution. (IPEDS will partially correct this problem.)

"The Annual Report on the Economic Status of the Profession" published by the American Association of University Professors (AAUP) provides the most timely and comprehensive data on instructional staff at the institutional level. This report includes an institutional classification, average salary and compensation by rank, a rating of average salary and compensation by rank, fringe benefits as a percentage of average salary, percentage of tenured faculty, percentage increase in salary, number of full-time faculty by rank and sex, and average salary by rank and sex. AAUP converts twelve-month salaries to the standard academic year basis when necessary and presents all data combined on the same basis.

The College and University Personnel Association (CUPA) publishes data annually on college and university administrators. In the "Administrative Compensation Survey" data are provided on ninety-four first-line administrative positions, such as chief executive officer, registrar, and director of institutional research. The "Administrative Compensation Survey Supplement" covers forty second-line administrative positions, including assistant to the president, manager of payroll, and director of the computer center. Both of these reports provide national-level data only, but salary data are broken down by institutional type, sector, size, and budget. Also, comparisons are provided between inside and outside hires, minorities and nonminorities, and years of service.

Tuition and Student Financial Aid. Table 3 lists data sources on tuition and student financial aid. Much of the data on tuition and fees is at the institutional level; student financial aid data tends to be reported at more aggregated levels.

The College Board annually publishes the *College Cost Book*, which is designed to help students plan for college. Over and above its intended use, this book can be extremely useful as a comparative data source on expenses at individual colleges and universities. In addition to tuition and fees, estimated costs for books and supplies, room and board, transportation, and other expenses are provided. This document is also a timely source, as it usually contains current year data.

The Center for Statistics is another major source of institutional-level data on tuition and required fees and room and board charges. These data are collected annually in the "Institutional Characteristics" survey. As with other HEGIS surveys, the timeliness of the data can be a problem.

Both the Southern Regional Education Board (SREB) and the Western Interstate Commission for Higher Education (WICHE) publish tuition and fee data by institution in a more timely fashion than HEGIS. The WICHE report also gives one-year and five-year percentage changes.

Students. As can be seen in Table 4, the student area encompasses several topics: enrollments, degrees awarded, the residence of students, high school graduates, and a number of longitudinal studies on students. Of these topics, data on enrollments, degrees awarded, and residence of students can be found at the institutional level. There are two frequently sought data elements that are not readily available: noncredit enrollment and student credit hours. However, beginning in 1987 student credit hours will be available through the IPEDS "Total Institutional Activity" survey. Noncredit enrollment is available for a large sample of public two-year colleges in the annual NACUBO study of two-year college finances (see Table 1).

Both the Center for Statistics and the College Board are sources of institutional enrollments by level, sex, and attendance status. In the HEGIS survey the full-time equivalent (FTE) enrollment is also given, and in even-numbered years, data are available by twelve major fields of study and by racial/ethnic category.

The HEGIS "Fall Enrollment Survey" and the College Board's "Annual Survey of Colleges" differ slightly in the definitions of full-time and part-time enrollment. HEGIS defines a full-time student as one whose academic load is at least 75 percent of the institution's normal full-time load. The College Board defines full-time enrollment as a minimum of thirty semester hours or forty-five quarter hours.

In a study of HEGIS enrollment data (Peng, 1979), the results indicated that the quality was generally quite good in the aggregate; error rates were typically less than 1 percent. At the disaggregated level, more than 25 percent of the institutions studied did not follow the classifications

Table 2. Staff and Personnel

TITLE	CONTENT	PUA*	FREQUENCY	SOURCE
Salaries, Tenure, and Fringe Benefits of Full-time Instructional Faculty	Full-time instructional faculty and salary outlay by rank, by sex, and by 9-month and 12-month contracts. Also includes expenditures for fringe benefits.	I	Annually as part of HEGIS. Will be continued in IPEDS biennially as "Salaries and Fringe Benefits".	Information Office Center for Statistics/OERI U. S. Department of Education 400 Maryland Avenue Washington, D. C. 20202 (800) 424-1616
Annual Report on the Economic Status of the Profession	Institutional classification, average salaries by rank, average compensation, benefits, salary increases, tenured faculty by rank, number of full-time faculty, and average salary by rank and sex.	IN	Annually.	American Association of University Professors 1012 14th Street N. W., Suite 500 Washington, D. C. 20005 (202) 737-5900 or (800) 424-2973
National Faculty Salary Survey by Discipline and Rank in State Colleges and Universities	Salary data for faculty in over 200 member schools of AASCU. Data are provided for most of the program areas in the classification of instructional programs at the two-digit level.	DI	Annually since 1981-82.	CUPA 11 Dupont Circle, Suite 120 Washington, D. C. 20036 (202) 462-1038
National Faculty Salary Survey by Discipline and Rank in Private Colleges and Universities	Salary data for faculty in over 450 private colleges. Data are provided for most of the program areas in the classification of instructional programs at the two-digit level.	DI	Annually since 1982-83.	CUPA 11 Dupont Circle, Suite 120 Washington, D. C. 20036 (202) 462-1038
Administrative Compensation Survey	Compilation of salaries paid at more than 1,400 institutions for 94 management positions. Data are cross-referenced and indexed according to enrollment, budget, region, type of institution, and public/private.	N	Annually since 1977-78.	CUPA 11 Dupont Circle, Suite 120 Washington, D. C. 20036 (202) 462-1038
Administrative Compensation Survey Supplement	Compensation data for 39 secondary administrative positions at over 1,350 institutions. For example, assistant to the president, director of student activities, and others.	N	Annually since 1982-83.	CUPA 11 Dupont Circle, Suite 120 Washington, D. C. 20036 (202) 462-1038
Equal Employment Opportunity Commission (EEO-6) Higher Education	Comprehensive data on all staff in postsecondary institutions with 15 or more full-time employees by status and position. Data collected prior to 1987 is available only at the national and state levels.	ISM	Biennially. Starting in 1987 the Center for Statistics (CS) will process the data for the EEOC. CS will distribute summary data.	Information Office Center for Statistics/OERI U. S. Department of Education 400 Maryland Avenue Washington, D. C. 20202 (800) 424-1616

Table 2. *(continued)*

Public Employment Series GE	Number of higher education instructional and other employees for state government and state and local government combined. Also provides payroll data for higher education instructional employees and other employees.	S	Annually.	Customer Services Section (Publications) Data User Services Division Bureau of the Census Washington, D. C. 20208-20233 (301) 763-4100
Survey of Scientific and Engineering Personnel Employed at Colleges and Universities	Headcounts of full- and part-time scientists and engineers by sex and field, highest degree earned, and estimates of the extent of R&D involvement on an FTE basis.	I	Periodically since 1954; annually since 1973.	NSF Division of Science Resources Studies 1800 G Street, N. W. Washington, D. C. 20550 (202) 634-4673

*Primary Unit of Analysis: D=Department or Discipline
I=Institutional
S=State
N=National

Table 3. Tuition and Student Financial Aid

TITLE	CONTENT	PUA*	FREQUENCY	SOURCE
College Cost Book	Tuition and fees at more than 3,000 colleges and universities recognized by the U. S. Department of Education, along with other data.	I	Annually as part of the Annual Survey of Colleges.	The College Board 45 Columbus Avenue New York, NY 10023-6917 (212) 713-8116
Institutional Characteristics of Colleges and Universities	Resident and nonresident tuition and required fees for undergraduate and graduate students; room and board charges; recognized accreditation; and descriptive information about the institution.	I	Annually except in 1982-83. In that year the Basic Student Charges Survey was substituted.	Information Office Center for Statistics U. S. Department of Education 400 Maryland Avenue Washington, D. C. 20202 (800) 424-1616
Basic Student Charges	Resident and nonresident tuition and required fees for undergraduate and graduate students; and room and board charges.	I	1982-83 only.	Information Office Center for Statistics U. S. Department of Education 400 Maryland Avenue Washington, D. C. 20202 (800) 424-1616
Resident and Nonresident Undergraduate and Graduate Tuition and/or Required Fees Public Universities, Colleges and State Universities, and Community Colleges: A National Comparison	Average tuition and/or required fees for public institutions reported by type of institution and state. One- and five-year percentage changes also reported.	S	Annually since 1968-69.	Washington Higher Education Coordinating Board 908 East Fifth Avenue, WE-II Olympia,WA 98504 (206) 753-2210
Tuition and Fees Southern Regional Education Board	Tuition and fees at institutions in the 15 Southern Regional Education Board (SREB) member states.	I	Annually.	SREB 1340 Spring Street, N. W. Atlanta, GA 30309 (404) 875-9211
Tuition and Fees in Public Higher Education in the West	Tuition and fees of the 14 Western Interstate Commission for Higher Education (WICHE) member states. Includes resident/nonresident and undergraduate/graduate at public 2-year and 4-year institutions. Periodically includes summaries of tuition policies.	I	Annually since 1977-78.	WICHE Information Clearinghouse P. O. Drawer P Boulder, CO 80301-9752 (303) 497-0200
National Student Financial Aid Study	National-level data on part-time/full-time students, aid-recipients/non-recipients in all types of postsecondary education.	N	Pilot study conducted in Winter 1985-86. Complete study in 1986-87.	Information Office Center for Statistics U. S. Department of Education 400 Maryland Avenue Washington, D. C. 20202 (800) 424-1616

Table 3. *(continued)*

NASSGP Annual Survey	Financial aid dollar amounts disbursed and types of financial aid programs available to students in each state. Comparative statistics for several types of programs are displayed in tabular and narrative form.	S	Annually since 1969-70.	Research Statistics Pennsylvania Higher Education Assistance Agency Towne House 660 Boas Street Harrisburg, PA 17102 (717) 257-2794
National Council of Higher Education Loan Programs, Inc. Guaranty Agency Survey	Information on student loan guaranty agency's operations and policies, organization and functions, finances, borrower characteristics, and loan volumes.	N	Annually since 1979.	New York State Higher Education Services Corp. Room 1438 Twin Towers 99 Washington Avenue Albany, NY 12255 (518) 474-8336

*Primary Unit of Analysis: D=Department or Discipline
I=Institution
S=State
N=National

Table 4. Students

TITLE	CONTENT	*PUA	FREQUENCY	SOURCE
High School Graduates: Projections for the Fifty States	Projections of high school graduates for each state, region of the country, and the nation. Detailed state-level data on which the projections are based are also included.	SN	Published in 1979 and 1984.	WICHE Publications Office P. O. Drawer P Boulder, CO 80301-9752 (303) 497-0290
Fall Enrollment in Institutions of Higher Education	Full-time/part-time enrollment of undergraduate, graduate, and first-professional students by sex. Every two years data are provided by racial/ethnic category. IPEDS will provide enrollment age interval every four years.	I	Annually as part of HEGIS. Will be continued in IPEDS.	Information Office Center for Statistics/OERI U. S. Department of Education 400 Maryland Avenue Washington, D. C. 20202 (800) 424-1616
Fall Enrollment	Full-time/part-time enrollment of undergraduate and graduate students by sex.	ISN	Annually as part of the Annual Survey of Colleges.	The College Board 45 Columbus Avenue New York, NY 10023-6917 (212) 713-8116
Fall Enrollment in Occupationally Specific Programs	Fall enrollment in occupationally specific programs at the sub-baccalaureate level at postsecondary institutions.	DI	Biennially beginning in 1987.	Information Office Center for Statistics/OERI U. S. Department of Education 400 Maryland Avenue Washington, D. C. 20202 (800) 424-1616
Residence and Migration of College Students	Number of first-time students enrolled at an institution by state of residence.	ISN	Biennially as part of HEGIS. Will be continued in IPEDS.	Information Office Center for Statistics/OERI U. S. Department of Education 400 Maryland Avenue Washington, D. C. 20202 (800) 424-1616
Degrees and Other Formal Awards Conferred	Number of degrees and other formal awards conferred by postsecondary institutions by program and sex. Data are available in odd numbered years by racial/ethnic category.	DI	Annually as part of HEGIS. Will be continued in IPEDS as "Completions".	Information Office Center for Statistics/OERI U. S. Department of Education 400 Maryland Avenue Washington, D. C. 20202 (800) 424-1616
Total Institutional Activity	Total credit/contact hours attempted at an institution. Hours are reported by course level for undergraduate, graduate, and professional students. Unduplicated headcount enrollment by student level is also reported.	ISN	Annually beginning in 1987 as part of IPEDS.	Information Office Center for Statistics/OERI U. S. Department of Education 400 Maryland Avenue Washington, D. C. 20202 (800) 424-1616

Table 4. *(continued)*

Cooperative Institutional Research Program	National data sample on incoming freshmen attitudes, values, and characteristics. Some senior followup research has been conducted.	N Annually.	Cooperative Institutional Research Program University of California Los Angeles, CA 90052 (213) 825-1925
High School and Beyond	A 1980 national data sample on high school students' experience in school and plans for the future. Also includes test scores.	N Base survey in 1980. Followup studies are done at two-year intervals.	Education Outcomes Division Center for Statistics/OERI U. S. Department of Education 400 Maryland Avenue Washington, D. C. 20202 (800) 424-1616
National Assessment of Educational Progress	Data on the knowledge and skills of 9, 13, 17- year olds and occasionally adults age 26-35. Learning areas include art, career and occupational development, citizenship/social studies, math, literature, science, and writing. Information on the respondent and school is included.	N Annually between 1969 and 1980. Biennially since 1980.	Education Outcomes Division Center for Statistics/OERI U. S. Department of Education 400 Maryland Avenue Washington, D. C. 20202 (800) 424-1616
National Education Longitudinal Study	Comparable to High School and Beyond but includes a postsecondary component of first-time students in college and in noncollegiate postsecondary institutions. Includes persistence, transfer, and withdrawls; student characteristics; financial aid; academic performance; and labor force participation. National and regional level data available.	N Base year will be 1990 as a continuation of NLS.	Education Outcomes Division Center for Statistics/OERI U. S. Department of Education 400 Maryland Avenue Washington, D. C. 20202 (800) 424-1616
Recent College Graduates	Study of bachelor's and master's degree recipients examining employment and salary in relation to major field of study. Special attention is given to graduates newly qualified to teach.	N Periodically.	Special Survey Branch Center for Statistics/OERI U. S. Department of Education 400 Maryland Avenue Washington, D. C. 20202 (800) 424-1616
Survey of Graduate Science and Engineering Students and Postdoctorates	Counts of full- and part-time graduate students with detailed information on sources of support, sex, level of study, citizenship, and race/ethnic category.	I Annually since 1972.	NSF Division of Science Resources Studies 1800 G Street, N. W. Washington, D. C. 20550 (202) 634-4673

*PUA=Primary Unit of Analysis: D=Department of Discipline
                              I=Institution
                              S=State
                              N=National

for student level. Firnberg and Christal (1984) found that many institutions included students in their enrollment counts that were supposed to be excluded; 26 percent included auditors and 63 percent included high school students. There is no reason to expect that the College Board's enrollment data would not have similar inaccuracies.

HEGIS is the only source for degrees-awarded data listed in Table 4. These data can be obtained at the institutional level by major field of study, sex, and racial/ethnic category in odd-numbered years. Peng also found that the quality of the degrees-awarded data was good with error rates at the aggregate level at less than 1 percent. However, problems appeared when disaggregation was taken to the level of program categories (for example, molecular biology) within major fields. Double majors also were the source of inconsistencies in classification from one institution to another.

The HEGIS "Residence and Migration" survey is the major source for this subject area. Since 1979 data have been collected on all first-time students enrolled in an institution by level, sex, and full-time or part-time status. Although as Table 4 indicates, these data are to be made available biennially. Unfortunately, between 1979 and 1984 a series of problems undermined the utility of the data. A nagging, and obviously fundamental, problem is how to determine student residence in a consistent manner.

Knowing the number of high school graduates can be extremely useful in enrollment projections. WICHE publishes these data by state, region, and the nation every several years. Projections are made for a period of seventeen to eighteen years hence, depending on the availability of data on resident live births.

Facility Operations and Libraries. The data for this area are not particularly abundant, as is evident from Table 5. Consequently, data on facilities and libraries may be most accessible from individual institutions.

Perhaps the best source for facility data is the Association of Physical Plant Administrators. This group surveys 750 colleges and universities biennially to collect data on the operating and maintenance costs of campus facilities. Information on the number and salaries of employees who work in plant maintenance operations are also provided.

The HEGIS "College and University Libraries" survey provides a comprehensive set of data on libraries. Included are counts of periodicals, books, government documents, microforms, and audiovisuals; circulations; staffing and salary data by sex; and expenditures by categories such as salaries, books, and binding.

Fact Books and Compendia. Some publications provide compendia about higher education such as directories and fact books. Table 6 lists a number of these sources. One of the advantages of this type of data source is that they often provide data that may not be available any other place. For example, the *Statistical Abstract* publishes enrollments and average

Table 5. Facility Operations and Libraries

TITLE	CONTENT	PUA*	FREQUENCY	SOURCE
The Comparative Costs and Staffing Survey	Data associated with the operating and maintenance costs of campus facilities for 750 schools. Energy costs are included in the 1984-85 report. Information is provided on FTE employees and salaries of 13 job functions related to facility management.	I	Biennially.	Association of Physical Plant Administrators of Colleges and Universities (APPA) 1446 Duke Street Alexandria, VA 22314-3492 (703) 684-1446
College and University Libraries	Data on the holdings, circulation, staffing, and finances of college libraries.	I	Biennially as part of HEGIS. Will be continued every four years in IPEDS.	Information Office Center for Statistics/OERI U. S. Department of Education 400 Maryland Avenue. Washington, D. C. 20202 (800) 424-1616
ARL Statistics	Data describe research library resources, expenditures, interlibrary loans, and staffing, as well as university enrollments, Ph.D.'s awarded, and Ph.D. fields for members of ARL.	I	Anually since 1974-75.	Association of Research Libraries 1527 New Hampshire Avenue N. W. Washington, D. C. 20036

*Primary Unit of Analysis: D=Department or Discipline
I=Institution
S=State
N=National

Table 6. Fact Book and Compendia of Resources

TITLE	CONTENT	*PUA	FREQUENCY	SOURCE
Higher Education Financing in the Fifty States	Comprehensive set of financial and supporting statistics on higher education. Data are provided by state, by type of institution, and by sector. Data include institutional financing, trend data, faculty salaries, enrollment data, and information on state funding. A commentary is also provided which highlights unique state conditions and accomplishments.	SN	Published for FY76, FY79, FY81, FY83, and FY84.	National Center for Higher Education Management Systems (NCHEMS) P. O. Drawer P Boulder, CO 80501
Digest of Education Statistics	Abstract of statistical information covering prekindergarten through graduate school. Tables related to higher education report enrollments, faculty/staff, institutions, degrees, income, student charges, financial aid, cost per student, expenditures, and property.	ISN	Annually since 1962 except for combined editions for 1977-78 and 1983-84.	Information Office Center for Statistics/OERI U. S. Department of Education 400 Maryland Avenue Washington, D. C. 20202 (800) 424-1616
Fact Book on Higher Education	Baseline and trend data on demographics, the economy, enrollments, institutions, faculty/staff, students, and earned degrees displayed in tables and charts.	SN	Annually since 1958.	Compiled by the American Council on Education (ACE) One Dupont Circle, Suite 800 Washington, D. C. 20036 (202) 833-4700 Published by MacMillan Publishing Co. 866 Third Avenue New York, NY 10022
Fact Book on Higher Education in the South	Data about each member state of the Southern Regional Board (SREB), and related regional and national averages. Includes population and the economy, enrollment and institutions, degrees, institutional finances, student finances and faculty.	S	Annually since 1964.	SREB 1340 Spring Street, N. W. Atlanta, GA 30309 (404) 875-9211
Facts about New England Colleges, Universities and Institutes	Enrollment and other characteristics of the institutions in the six member states of the New England Board of Higher Education.	S	Annually.	NEBHE 45 Temple Place Boston, MA 02111 (617) 357-9620
Digest of Statistics on Higher Education in the United States	Data on institutions, enrollment, public/private and 4-year/2-year ratios, faculty/staff, and current fund expenditures and ratios.	N	Annually	TIAA/CREF Educational Research Division 730 Third Avenue New York, NY 10017

Table 6. (continued)

Title	Description	Primary Unit of Analysis*	Frequency	Source/Ordering
Community, Technical and Junior College Directory	Data on 1,219 accredited two-year colleges. Includes name, address, phone number, chief executive officer, accreditation status, type of academic year, enrollment, faculty/staff, and tuition and fees.	I	Annually.	AACJC Publication Sales 80 South Early Street Alexandria, VA 22304 (703) 823 6966
Education Directory, Colleges and Universities	Includes phone number, address, county, FICE code, date established, enrollment, tuition and fees, calendar, control or affiliation, highest level of offering, type of program, classification, and accreditation. Appendixes have changes (e.g. new campuses, mergers, closures).	I	Annually.	Information Office Center for Statistics/OERI U. S. Department of Education 400 Maryland Avenue Washington, D. C. 20202 (800) 424-1616
HEP Higher Education Directory	Includes institutional characteristics such as phone number, address, highest offering, accreditation, and administrative officers.	I	Annually.	Higher Education Publications, Inc. 1302 18th Street, N. W., Suite 401 Washington, D. C. 20036 (202) 296-9106
The Condition of Education	Includes elementary, secondary, and higher education. Higher education covers enrollment, faculty, finance, and degrees.	N	Annually.	Compiled by the Center for Statistics. Published by Superintendent of Documents U. S. Government Printing Office Washington, D. C. 20402 (202) 783-3238
The College Handbook	Includes enrollments, freshman class profile, campus location, majors, freshman and transfer admissions, tuition and fees, financial aid, student activities, athletics, and housing.	I	Annually.	College Board Publication Orders Box 886 New York, NY 10101
Statistical Abstract of the United States	One chapter is devoted to education and includes enrollments, student financial assistance, tenure, degrees earned, libraries, test scores, and noncollegiate postsecondary data.	N	Annually since 1878.	U. S. Government Printing Office Washington, D. C. 20402 (202) 783-3238

*Primary Unit of Analysis: D=Department or Discipline
I=Institutions
S=State
N=National

tuition by program for noncollegiate postsecondary schools. The data in some of the published reports (for example, *Condition of Education* and *Digest of Education Statistics*) are highly aggregated, but they do provide some institutional norms for comparative purposes.

The College Handbook published by the College Board is a quick reference to many data elements for colleges and universities. Included are data on enrollments, programs offered, tuition and fees, admissions selectivity, housing, and so on. For admissions evaluation, comparative data on number of applicants, acceptances, and enrollees can be quite useful. Data on SAT and ACT scores as well as class rank for entering freshmen are provided for many institutions.

The American Association of Community and Junior Colleges publishes annually the *Community, Junior, and Technical College Directory* with the address, chief executive officer, credit enrollment, tuition and fees, and number of faculty (full- and part-time), professional staff, and administrators. Community education enrollment—students participating in noncredit activities—is also provided.

NCHEMS *Higher Education Financing in the Fifty States, Interstate Comparisons* provides a wealth of information organized at the state level. This study organizes a comprehensive set of state-level financial and supporting statistics on higher education, including a profile of each state's population, tax structure, and the amount allocated to higher education. Enrollment, finance, and faculty salary data are provided by state and by type of institution. A variety of measures are used, such as absolute amounts, percent distribution, constant dollars, and indexes with respect to the U.S. average. A commentary for each state highlights unique state conditions and accomplishments.

Other Data Sources. There is a growing cadre of organizations that provide access to data bases for a fee either through special hard-copy reports, or in machine-readable form for use on a computer. A number of these organizations are included in Table 7. Often detailed data by institution are made available that are not published elsewhere. The organizations can sometimes display data in the manner in which a client specifies.

Many states now maintain extensive data bases on their public institutions and sometimes data on private institutions as well. In some instances, the state data base coincides with HEGIS data. In other cases, state data may be more or less detailed and may include data elements different from those used in HEGIS. In pursuing state-level data, it is often worthwhile to contact coordinating agencies or system-level boards of regents or trustees.

The nation's three regional higher education associations (SREB, WICHE, and NEBHE) are also sources of comparative data. These organizations are especially useful for interstate comparisons in their respective regions but generally less so for interinstitutional comparisons.

Table 7. Organizations

ORGANIZATION	SERVICES
Information Office Center for Statistics/OERI U. S. Department of Education 400 Maryland Avenue Washington, D. C. 20202 (800) 424-1616	Publications and data tapes of statistical data collected in the national surveys of postsecondary institutions by the Center for Statistics.
NCHEMS P. O. Drawer P Boulder, CO 80301 (303) 497-0301	Standard and custom reports on a variety of statistical data about higher education. Most reports use the HEGIS surveys. Peer-group selection is also available.
NACUBO Financial Management Center One Dupont Circle, Suite 500 Washington, D. C. 20036-1178 (202) 861-2535	Comparative financial statistics of selected institutions drawn from the data base for the report "Comparative Financial Statistics for Community and Junior Colleges".
Maryse Eymonerie Associates P. O. Box 520 McLean, VA 22101 (703) 448-8815	Selected faculty salary tables drawn from the data base for the report "The Annual Report on the Economic Status of the Profession" published by the American Association of University Professors.
The College Board Data Services 45 Columbus Avenue New York, NY 10023-6917 (212) 713-8116	Specialized tabulations of enrollments and tuition drawn from the Annual Survey of Colleges.
CUPA Eleven Dupont Circle, Suite 120 Washington, D. C. 20036 (202) 462-1038	Standardized and special studies and analyses of data from "Administrative Compensation Survey" and supplement and "National Faculty Salary Survey by Discipline and Rank in Private Colleges and Universities" and "National Faculty Salary Survey by Discipline and Rank in State Colleges and Universities".
John Minter Associates 2400 Central Avenue, Suite B-2 Boulder, CO 80301 (303) 499-8110	Fifty different ratios for 3,200 colleges. Includes revenue, expenditure, net operating, asset, debt, enrollment, Pell grants, and tuition.

Numerous special interest associations gather and maintain data on individual institutions or can at least provide normative data by type of institution. These sources include at least the following (and there may be others):

American Association of Colleges of Nursing
American Association of Community and Junior Colleges
American Association of Medical Colleges
American Association of State Colleges and Universities
American Association of University Professors
Association of American Universities
Association of Physical Plant Administrators

Association of Research Libraries
College and University Personnel Association
College and University Systems Exchange
Council for Financial Aid to Education
Council of Graduate Schools
National Association of Independent Colleges and Universities
National Association of State Universities and Land-Grant
    Colleges
National Association of Trade and Technical Schools
National League of Nursing.

Access to the data maintained by these associations, both regional and special interest, can be obtained through their publications or through direct request.

Several universities gather and make available particular kinds of comparative data, including the University of Alabama (statistics on schools of education), Oklahoma State University (faculty salaries for a sample of state colleges and universities), and the University of Arkansas (administrative salaries at doctorate-granting universities).

Various special surveys are published that occasionally contain normative data useful for comparison purposes. The *Chronicle of Higher Education* is a handy source for synopses of these studies and for a variety of specially commissioned surveys. The American Council on Education (ACE) uses a panel of institutions for surveys on issues of current interest; results are available in ACE publications.

The largest collection of literature on higher education is found in the Educational Resources Information Center (ERIC) system. Although it is not a major source of comparative data, the ERIC collection contains numerous one-time studies, some of which contain data potentially useful for comparative purposes. It is a primary source for data about student attrition and retention where no national survey data are available.

Conclusion

A basic premise of this chapter is that there is a growing demand for comparative data. Accordingly, efforts should be made to enhance the utility and minimize the risks of using comparative data. Maintaining data quality should be a shared responsibility. Institutional officials can insist that external agencies make adequate efforts to ensure that the data they collect and report meet appropriate standards for validity and accuracy. Institutions themselves should be willing to assist in identifying data quality problems (Hyatt, 1982). Often the source of bad data about an institution is the institution itself. By working together, there will be enhanced prospects for quality data and for maximum utility of comparative data.

References

Andrew, L., Fortune, J., and McCluskey, L. *Analysis of Uses of HEGIS Data.* Blacksburg: College of Education, Virginia Polytechnic Institute and State University, 1980.

Brinkman, P., and Krakower, J. *Comparative Data for Administrators in Higher Education.* Boulder, Colo.: National Center for Higher Education Management Systems, 1983.

Firnberg, J. W., and Christal, M. E. "HEGIS Data: Is What You See What You Get?" *College and University,* 1984, *60* (1), 21–31.

Hyatt, J. A. "Using National Financial Data for Comparative Analysis." In C. Frances (ed.), *Successful Responses to Financial Difficulty.* New Directions for Higher Education, no. 38. San Francisco: Jossey-Bass, 1982.

Lapovsky, L. "The Utility of HEGIS Data in Making Interinstitutional Comparisons." Paper prepared for Maryland State Board of Higher Education, Annapolis, August 1983.

Minter, W. J., and Conger, C. A. "Comparing Institutional Reports of HEGIS Financial Data with AICPA–NACUBO Standards." *Business Officer,* March 1979a, pp. 18–20.

Minter, W. J., and Conger, C. A. "Comparing Institutional Reports of HEGIS Financial Data with AICPA–NACUBO Standards—Part Two." *Business Officer,* April 1979b, pp. 18–20.

Minter, W. J., and Conger, C. A. "Comparing Institutional Reports of HEGIS Financial Data with AICPA–NACUBO Standards—Part Three." *Business Officer,* May 1979c, pp. 16–18.

Patrick, C., and Collier, D. J. "Checking the Validity of Summary Statistics from HEGIS Financial Data." In C. Frances and S. L. Coldren (eds.), *Assessing Financial Health.* New Directions for Higher Education, no. 26. San Francisco: Jossey-Bass, 1979.

Peng, S. S. *HEGIS Post-Survey Validation Study.* Summary Report. Rockville, Md.: WESTAT, 1979.

Wittstruck, J. "Survey of Automated Data Collections and SHEEO Agency Use of Microcomputers and Related Software." Denver, Colo.: State Higher Education Executive Officers, 1985.

Melodie E. Christal is director of administration at the National Center for Higher Education Management Systems, Boulder, Colorado.

John R. Wittstruck is director, State Higher Education Executive Officers/Center for Statistics Communication Network, Denver, Colorado.

Setting up a successful data-sharing project involves commonsense guidelines: Be clear what you want, take advantage of what already exists, use appropriate technology, staff adequately, recognize that each institution is different, and concentrate on achieving insight rather than precision.

Setting Up
a Data-Sharing Project

John A. Dunn, Jr.

Data sharing and comparative studies support college and university planning and management by enriching the context for decision making.

As individuals, we exist in a social context; we understand our abilities and our history in comparison to others, and, at least to some extent, we shape our future based on that context. Institutions do the same. Whether as independent colleges or statewide systems, each tries to fulfill its particular mission. But each exists in a context of competition for faculty, students, and resources.

As with individuals, all types of interinstitutional comparisons are useful—to peers, to those one wishes to emulate, to one's neighbors. Since we have different abilities, aspire to different ends, and are at various stages of development, our comparisons must take into account these factors.

Many institutions find it most useful to systematize much of their comparative work through some formal arrangement. Some of the current data-sharing consortia and practical considerations for setting up such arrangements are discussed here.

The author wishes to express appreciation to Patrick T. Terenzini for suggesting the concept of this chapter and to Larry H. Litten, Mark Meredith, and Thomas J. Abdella for helpful reviews of the outline.

P. T. Brinkman (ed.). *Conducting Interinstitutional Comparisons.*
New Directions for Institutional Research, no. 53. San Francisco: Jossey-Bass, Spring 1987.

Ongoing Data-Sharing Consortia

It is useful to distinguish among three types of data-collection activities. First, there are required or voluntary data-collection activities organized by the federal government, the states, or state systems of higher education. The most important of these are the federal Higher Education General Information surveys (HEGIS), which is soon to be the Integrated Postsecondary Data System (IPEDS), organized by the Center for Education Statistics, which was formerly the National Center for Education Statistics, of the Department of Education. The second are voluntary single-purpose surveys conducted usually by noninstitution-based professional organizations. Among these are the "Voluntary Support of Education" survey by the Council on Financial Aid to Education (CFAE), the "Comparative (Endowment) Performance" study by the National Association of College and University Business Officers (NACUBO), salary surveys by the College and University Personnel Association (CUPA), and library surveys by the Association of Research Libraries and the Association of College Research Libraries. A third category are voluntary associations of institutions for the purpose of exchanges of data and cooperative studies. This is the category with which this chapter is primarily concerned.

The lines among these categories should not be drawn too sharply. NACUBO draws heavily on institutional personnel to conduct its endowment study; some voluntary associations, like the Consortium on Financing Higher Education (COFHE), have separately incorporated; all tend to use each others' data when possible.

The four key characteristics of the third category of data-exchange activities are that (1) they are voluntary, (2) they usually have few, if any, full-time personnel, (3) they are directed by the concerns of their members, and (4) institutional representatives often take on membership in addition to their regular activities. The guidelines outlined in this chapter indicate what it is realistic to expect from activities of this nature.

Advantages of these voluntary data-sharing endeavors are that they can (1) reduce redundancy of effort in that they avoid repetitive requests for similar information, (2) spread the cost of high-risk, long-term high-cost survey projects, and (3) enhance the legitimacy of certain projects or efforts, both on campus and externally.

Typical of these organizations are the following:

1. The Association of American Universities Data Exchange (AAUDE). Organized in 1973, the AAUDE is a voluntary, year-round effort with a current membership of thirty-three private and public AAU institutions. AAUDE has no formal connection with the office of the AAU and is coordinated by the University of Colorado, Boulder, by Mark Meredith. The purpose of the AAUDE is to exchange annually recurring data as well as nonrecurring special survey data. Institutional representatives meet annually.

2. The Consortium on Financing Higher Education (COFHE). With a current membership of thirty leading independent national-draw colleges and universities, COFHE is a separately incorporated consortium that grew out of the 1972 Sloan Foundation Study Group. A small central staff headed by Katherine Hanson and Larry H. Litten works out of offices in Cambridge, Massachusetts, and Washington, D.C. COFHE conducts annual surveys in such areas as admissions, financial aid, and costs; directs special studies at the request of the members; and monitors federal and independent-sector developments.

3. The Tufts-EDUCOM data-sharing project now involves fifteen universities and forty-five colleges. Participants contribute information on a wide variety of institutional activities (finances, enrollments, admissions, libraries, space, personnel, and so on) to a shared data base using EDUCOM's Higher Education Data-Sharing Service (HEDS). Institutions can then extract raw data as well as a wide variety of trend indicators, ratios, and other analyses. This information is available both in report form and in a format for further local microcomputer analysis. Key personnel are Daniel A. Updegrove at EDUCOM, and John A. Dunn, Jr., and Thomas J. Abdella at Tufts.

4. The Urban 13 was started over twenty years ago by the vice presidents of a number of public urban-based institutions in the Midwest and Northeast. In more recent years, the academic officers have been meeting twice a year to exchange information in a totally informal way on matters of common concern, such as retention, leaves, security, and so on. Last year, at the request of Nancy Avakian of the University of Misssouri, St. Louis, the institutional researchers at these universities started a series of meetings with the intent of establishing a more systematic data exchange.

5. The Southern University Group of 25, referred to as the SUG25 (despite having twenty-six members at the present time), is made up primarily of major public universities in the Southern Regional Education Board (SREB) region. It originated over sixteen years ago from one of the first institutional research workshops sponsored by the Association for Institutional Research, SREB, and Louisiana State University (LSU). Its major purpose is to share and exchange data in an informal and confidential manner. The groups meets twice annually to exchange ideas and studies and to discuss topics of current interest and concern. It exchanges certain data on faculty, students, and finances on a regular basis. Various members share the leadership for these projects. The SUG25 is currently chaired by Jerry Baudin at LSU. Allan Bloom at Virginia Polytechnic Institute (VPI) has been active in working toward computerization of the teacher-load data-exchange effort.

6. MINDS (the Multipurpose Interactive Database System) is a ten-year-old data-sharing service for the 105 Methodist colleges and universities

in the United States and is staffed by Ken Yamada at the Division of Higher Education of the United Methodist Church, Nashville. Data are collected from audited financial reports and an annual questionnaire; this data is then analyzed and reported back to each institution in the form of a two-page confidential summary of institutional health, and the mean data for all member schools is grouped in the five Carnegie Commission classifications.

(This is a partial listing; our apologies to many other endeavors for not including them due to lack of space.)

Starting a Comparison or Data-Sharing Project

The basic rule in starting such a project is to be as clear as possible at the outset about what the goal is of the data exchange. With this point established, then make all the decisions about membership, areas of data to share, project staffing, technology, and so on based on that understanding.

Membership. You would not be contemplating an information exchange project if you did not want to compare some aspect of your operation to that of other schools. The usefulness of this comparison depends directly on whether those who will use the data accept the other institutions as being sufficiently similar or as undergoing sufficiently similar pressures to constitute valid comparisons.

There are many ways to categorize colleges and universities for the purpose of comparative study: the Carnegie or NCHEMS classifications, peer groups, aspiration groups, regional groups, admissions competition groups, and so on. (The techniques for selecting peer institutions were reviewed in Chapter One.)

The key element in membership selection is to understand what you want the data for and to choose institutions that are valid comparisons for that purpose. In general, the more homogenous the group (in size, control, mission, program mix, wealth), the less significant the comparability problems will be (although these problems will never disappear).

Since the data exchange is a voluntary activity, you will also want to seek out among the comparable institutions those that want to participate.

Data to Exchange. Keep it simple, and start small. Be sure that those who want the data (typically, senior decision makers) specify what is needed in operational terms. You may need to help understand the availability of the data sought in your own institution as well as at others.

There is an almost infinite variety of interesting data. You will have to make an effort to keep the collection manageably small and focused on decision-oriented items. Take maximum advantage of what already exists. Resist the temptation to invest in tailor-made data definitions, unless you find that you cannot get "ready-to-wear" data anywhere. Find out about existing data exchanges and data collection activities, join them, and build on their work. See, for instance, the work of the AAU Data Exchange, especially with respect to faculty salaries; Dennis Jones's work at NCHEMS for the Council of Post-Secondary Accrediting Agencies; the data collections already being carried on by your state coordinating commission and the regional accrediting group; the NACUBO surveys of two-year colleges; the HEGIS (soon to be IPEDS) federal surveys; the AAUP faculty salary surveys; the ARL/ACRL library surveys; the CFAE surveys of "Voluntary Support of Education"; the NACUBO "Comparative Endowment Performance" studies; the ratios in the NACUBO "Financial Self-Assessment Workbook," soon to be updated, and their counterparts in the Peat, Marwick, Mitchell *Ratio Analysis in Higher Education* (1980). A more complete list of available sources is given in Chapter Two.

Technology. Use technology for data collection that is appropriate to your purpose. Do not get carried away with complex technology when something simpler will serve as well.

Telephone calls are remarkably time effective for one-shot surveys, especially where you distribute a questionnaire ahead of time so the respondent has time to gather the information being sought. Electronic mail provides a helpful variant, permitting time shifting by the respondents and avoiding telephone "tag."

Written surveys are very cost effective, since they allow respondents to answer at their own time convenience. These surveys lend themselves best to a situation where someone will do further analysis on behalf of the group and then write a report to the contributors. Electronic conferencing or bulletin boards provide many of the same benefits without the final write-up or report.

There is also data-base technology available that can be effective in allowing many institutions to contribute to and draw from a shared pool. The best of these is the EDUCOM Higher Education Data-Sharing System (HEDS) currently used by the Tufts-EDUCOM data-sharing project. This approach should be considered where

1. You wish to capture and hold an array of data but are not likely to think in advance of all the relationships that might prove interesting,
2. You and others wish to refer to the data base repetitively (such as for annual updates),
3. You wish to use the data base in different ways (such as to show trends over time for an institution, data in a particular area for all institutions for one year, or one data element for many institutions over time),
4. Institutions will wish to use the data base for different purposes at different times of year (in this case written reports would not be ideal), and

5. Users need only supply the raw data and have trend analyses, ratios, and other indicators computed centrally.

You should consider whether on-line access to the data base or batch input and retrieval of the data are desired. This question relates to the broader one of whether members need or should have direct access to the data base or whether it is more practical and economical for a coordinator to manipulate the data base. Finally, you will need to see what equipment and telecommunications facilities the prospective members have or are willing to acquire to support the project.

Staffing. In a voluntary data exchange, you can usually count on the institutional representatives to take on the work of collecting and submitting their school's data, but you will need someone responsible for organizing and supporting the effort.

If you use telephone surveys or questionnaires, someone must develop the instrument, distribute it, collect the responses, analyze them, write them up, and distribute the findings. This work may be shared among members, but such an arrangement, over time, usually proves less useful than having staff support.

If you use electronic technology in your data exchange, be sure there is a user-support person available *at all times* to answer questions. Technology evolves rapidly, so continuous training is needed; also, institutions will use different equipment, the host computer will make changes in its operating systems, and so forth. The staff person does not necessarily have to dedicate full-time attention to the project, but he or she must be available when a contributor calls with a problem. If not, the contributor will become discouraged and put aside the project in favor of something more interesting, more urgent, and easier to do. Over time, this steady succession of problems and postponements will erode the momentum of the project.

Basic Considerations

Comparisons Are Back-Burner Projects. Institutional comparisons and data-sharing projects can yield a better understanding of your institution over its own history and in comparison to others. The results of such comparisons provide a backdrop for decisions; they do not provide answers or ¬make decisions.

Outcomes of the studies tend to be viewed as interesting and helpful but not essential. These projects are therefore seldom assigned as a top priority. Further, since they tend to be laborious and have a long pay-off time, researchers often do not enlist them.

There are several steps for counterbalancing these institutional realities, as follows:

1. Seek to minimize the work involved. Do not invent anything (new definitions, new technology) if you do not have to. Choose the simplest way to get effective answers.

2. Make the data exchange project as interesting as possible. If you employ a new technology, use the process to help participants expand or update their skills. If you have conferences to agree on projects, present other materials at the same time.

3. Make sure there is someone who takes the lead, who feels responsible for the whole enterprise, and whom the group holds responsible for the success or failure of the project. Make sure that this individual has the time to work on the project to draft definitions, arrange meetings, support the technology, interpret the findings, and so on.

4. Start with modest ambitions. Then build on success with small items and do something more useful.

5. Make membership in the group voluntary but establish clear expectations of the members. You may have to provide ways of enforcing compliance by revoking membership, excluding others from access to data, and so on.

The Comparability Problem. Institutions really do differ. Even when differences are minor, each college or university insists on viewing itself as unique in at least some area. Therefore,

1. Do not oversell the data exchange project. There will always be questions about true comparability, and these should be recognized from the outset.

2. Concentrate on trends, ratios, distributions, and indicators, not on raw data. You are seeking insight, not numbers. (If your user group is composed of institutional researchers or other data handlers, you may want to concentrate on providing comparable raw data so they can make their own conclusions. Even in this case, however, do not overlook the power of indicators.)

3. Recognize that much of the value in the exercise will result from an orderly collection and analysis of your own data. Although this statement may be somewhat less true of major institutions with long-standing institutional research offices than for small colleges, it will usually prove to be the case.

4. Resist the temptation to force institutions into groups. Instead, try to set up useful data bases that each institution can use as desired to compare itself to X and Y institutions on some characteristics and to Z and Q institutions on others.

5. Involve the participants in questions of membership, data to collect, appropriate technology, definitions, use and control of information, and other key policy questions. The more homogeneous the group, the fewer the problems of comparability will be (although these issues may nevertheless be hotly contended).

To address the noncomparability problem, ask what the information will be used for and then collect data accordingly.

For areas where you need very specific data (salary comparisons to be used to attract or fund faculty), go to the microscopic level. The AAUDE, for instance, collects faculty salary data by subdiscipline and by rank. Do not attempt to aggregate these data. Leave them in full detail so that the other contributing institutions, which may not be organized the same way or which may have the same array of fields, can still use the information.

In all other areas use the highest level of aggregation that will give you reasonable approximations. For instance, if you want to know the total amount of restricted financial aid gifts, you probably do not need an analysis of the range of such awards or their origin.

Suggestions

There are a number of practical considerations that, if appropriately recognized, can help make a data-sharing activity productive.

1. Do not oversell the project. To get a project started, you will often need support from those in charge of the organization, the senior decision makers who will eventually use the information. It will take a couple of years of work, however, before you begin to have results that justify the time committed to the project.

2. Use your ingenuity in keeping participants' attention on the project. Formal memoranda of understanding can document initial intentions, but newsletters, regularly scheduled conferences, and many telephone calls can help keep the project on the front burner.

3. Respect each institution's ego needs. Your considering another school a peer does not mean that the institution feels similarly. Recognize that each institution will use the comparison data for its own political ends. This reality argues strongly for organizing data in such a way that each institution can select its comparison institutions and the areas, elements, and purpose of the comparison.

4. Early on in the activity, explicitly address questions of confidentiality and control of the data. Who can have access to institutional data? May the data be used outside the group? May individual institutions be identified or only the group as a whole?

5. Except where very detailed data are needed, use the highest useful levels of aggregation of data. The trade-off between the benefits of adding detail to achieve more comparability and the costs and problems of increasing data collection and entry indicates the need for a balance up the scale toward aggregation.

6. The comparative data will have served their purpose if they call attention to differences. You can then call your colleague with the differing data to check whether the differences are real or are figments of the definitions and, if they are real, to see what the underlying factors may be. If you find something of special interest, undertake a one-time study. Resist

the temptation to build into the system all the detail on every area you might want if differences were to emerge.

7. Even though trend analyses are extremely useful, minimize expectations for initial input of historical data. The older the data, the less likely they are to be either comparable or relevant to present decisions. The Tufts-EDUCOM project asks new members to input data for the last year and, if possible, the prior year. If institutions have good historical data, they can enter them; if not, starting with good recent data establishes a baseline for future comparisons.

8. Recognize that many of the benefits of the data-sharing project will come from by-products of the process. It will be useful to organize your own institution's data in a systematic way and subject them to careful trend and ratio analysis. Increased contact with colleagues at other institutions will yield ideas and insights. This increased communication will, in fact, be so important that you should take steps to facilitate it by instituting electronic mail systems, regular conferences, newsletters, and so on.

9. Finally, realize that there will be turnover in personnel at the member institutions and changes in institutional priorities. You will need to provide a continued retraining of participants and a continued reinforcement of the value of the enterprise as senior staff changes.

Summary

Remember that the purpose of the data-sharing project is insight, not data dictionaries or reams of printouts. The latter are indispensable, but they are tools, not products. Think through what you want; recognize that the effort takes time and support; where possible, use what already exists rather than inventing a new system or definition set; and seek to maximize communication rather than data generation.

Reference

Minter, J., Nelson, C. A., and Robinson, D. D. *Ratio Analysis in Higher Education.* New York: Peat, Marwick, Mitchell, 1980.

John A. Dunn, Jr., is vice-president for planning, Tufts University.

The popularity of the peer comparison method as a tool for decision making at all levels of the college or university often raises a number of issues. This chapter presents a model that systematically incorporates peer comparisons throughout the institutional planning cycle, alleviating a number of problems and increasing the power of comparison as a higher education management tool.

Institutional Uses of Comparative Data

Meredith A. Whiteley, Frances K. Stage

A peer comparison is a powerful tool in managing change within a college or university. From trustees to librarians, those involved at all levels of decision making are using peer comparisons to guide and direct change in colleges and universities around the country.

As the use of peer comparisons becomes more prevalent in internal institutional decision making, a number of issues emerge. One common issue on many campuses is the lack of agreement about who are the college or university's peers. Debate over peer selection is complicated further by the lack of a widely accepted peer selection methodology as well as the incomparability or unavailability of data from potential peer institutions. Due to these complications, the process of choosing an institution's peers frequently takes one of three paths: (1) Peers are imposed on the institution by the statewide governing board; (2) each unit or department independently selects its peers on the basis of its own, often unstated, criteria; or (3) peers are selected ad hoc by one administrative unit (typically the budget or legislative liaison office) and imposed on the rest of the institution. The first path seldom takes into consideration institution-specific program concerns. The second path results in a chaotic proliferation of peer comparisons that detracts from the credibility of comparisons. The third course runs counter to the spirit of collegiality as well as the goal of

P. T. Brinkman (ed.). *Conducting Interinstitutional Comparisons.*
New Directions for Institutional Research, no. 53. San Francisco: Jossey-Bass, Spring 1987.

increased faculty involvement in planning and evaluation that is the heart of the new direction in accreditation criteria (see for example, Southern Association . . . , 1984).

In addition to the question of who are peers is the equally thorny issue of what is a valid use of peer comparisons. Peer comparisons are used to support every management decision from justifying budget requests to providing operational models for collections. Further, much of what are called peer comparisons in higher education management are aimed not at implementing change but at defending past decisions. Users of peer comparisons frequently compile comparisons as an afterthought in order to develop accountability measures that are often divorced from the institution's goals and objectives. Whether or not these are valid uses of the comparative method is questionable.

Part of the problem in defining the valid uses of peer comparisons in institutional decision making resides in the fact that there is little theory to guide consideration of the purpose and parameters of comparisons. Further, development of the comparative method in higher education has been outside the context of the broader theories of comparative analysis in political science, sociology, and comparative education. As a result, the "valid" peer comparison in higher education frequently is addressed in primarily operational rather than substantive terms. However, as the use of peer comparisons becomes more popular and peer comparisons become more integrated into both internal and external institutional decision-making processes, there is increasing demand for a framework to guide the selection and use of effective peer comparisons.

Problems with Peer Comparisons

Looking across the administrative activities of a college or university, we find peer comparisons used simultaneously at multiple points throughout the organization. Faced with fiscal constraints and the corresponding demands for accountability, college and university administrators at all levels are searching for measures, norms, and models to guide decision making on an increasingly wide range of institutional management issues. Comparisons often are used to justify departmental budget requests, index salaries, allocate space, establish curriculum, and redesign administrative operations.

Part of the impetus for the proliferation of peer comparisons is external. College and university administrators, from central administration to individual departments, frequently assume the role of data suppliers and feed the growing appetite for comparative data of federal, state, and voluntary organizations. The use of this data by external agencies fosters an increased reliance on peer comparisons by college and university administrators in the internal decision-making processes. Yet, the use of peer comparisons raises several issues for the individual institution, its administration, and its faculty.

Diversity. The use of comparisons frequently raises philosophical issues regarding diversity and the role that peer comparisons play in the homogenization of American colleges and universities. As Birnbaum (1983) notes, institutional diversity is "one of the major ideological pillars of American higher education" (p. ix). Yet, colleges and universities are said to be moving increasingly away from their unique qualities and toward a homogenization of institutional purpose and form (Birnbaum, 1983; Jencks and Reisman, 1977; Newman, 1971).

The truth is that peer comparisons frequently are used as tools in this homogenization process. Although often unstated but implied, the purpose underlying many administrators' use of peer comparisons is to identify and then correct the differences between their institution and the norm of one or two national models. Within this context, differences are viewed as undesirable, a sign of inefficiency, of backwardness, or of failure.

Part of the problem is the tendency on the part of many administrators to look only at the mean of the peer group and not the range among the peers. If, for example, peer institutions A through F have a mean study space of 115 sq. ft./student FTE, those involved in decision making at institution G may see their institution as not in accord with 130 sq. ft./student FTE. Viewed simplistically, the obvious decision for some may be for institution G to reallocate part of its study space to other uses, regardless of the consideration that additional study space may be a necessary element in the institution's unique programming and quality.

However, the use of peer institution comparisons in this manner is only a symptom and not a cause of the failure on the part of many higher education administrators to recognize the unique roles of their institutions. These administrators lead their institutions in an uncoordinated fashion to assume all roles and all missions and use comparisons haphazardly to support simultaneous moves in several directions.

The fault is not in the method but in its application. Historically, informal institutional comparisons were a critical component in the development of a diverse array of American colleges and universities. Although new colleges and universities frequently were modeled after older, reputable institutions, such comparisons resulted in both a standardization and a diversity among colleges and universities. Founders of new colleges and universities were able to identify more clearly the elements they wished to emulate in their new institutions as well as those elements that would define their uniqueness (Brubacher and Rudy, 1976).

Currently, comparison and emulation are still components that are crucial in institutional strategic planning. Comparisons can provide a basis for the rational evaluation of differences and of similarities among institutions as well as the identification of diverse markets and niches.

Validity. Even when administrators are aware of the unique roles their institutions play, there are other problem areas. The actual mechanics involved in conducting a peer comparison can create problems of validity. Further, the use of data that are not comparable and controversy over variables and selection techniques can invalidate peer comparison.

Incomparability of data can exist in several different dimensions. Different histories, organizations, missions, and reporting systems can all produce unmatching data. Although external agencies who use comparative data have attempted to standardize data definitions and classifications across institutions, glaring problems still remain. Differences in the way institutions budget funds, finance projects, and classify departments lead to problems in interpreting data from two or more institutions. For example: (1) Inconsistencies in the way professional schools, such as law and medicine, are budgeted and reported often result in data that are incomparable (Hyatt and Thompson, 1980); (2) differences in the way institutions finance capital projects, either through direct appropriations or revenue bonds, are a threat to valid comparisons, and differences in bonding are usually not reflected in surveys (Lingenfelter, 1983); (3) some institutions that are well established have little need for major capital outlay, and their inclusion in a financial comparison may cause newer institutions with heavy capital outlays to appear inefficient; (4) state benefits often do not flow through institutional accounts, and institutions may receive state funds through appropriation structures, such as public health agencies, for laboratories and indigent care facilities, which may go unreported and thus skew comparisons (Hyatt, 1982).

Even when data are "clean" and the figures comparable, other questions arise. There is little agreement as to which variables are most appropriate for actual peer selection. The administrator must choose from a range of data that are accessible such as that on finances, faculty, students, and curricula, to data that are less accessible, such as the technological needs of area industry, economic conditions, alumni support, local politics, and regulatory restrictions. Those conducting peer selections to date primarily utilize the most accessible data, unintentionally neglecting many environmental factors critical to the development of institutions and the management of change.

A final, but critical, consideration in the attempt to construct a valid comparison is the method of selection. Commonly used techniques range from such questionable practices as basing selection strictly on athletic conference memberships (or other convenient groupings) to carefully devised algorithms that combine both quantitative and qualitative considerations. Major selection methods can be categorized into one of these major types.

Although examples of such problems abound (Harris, 1973), the intention is not to frighten administrators away from comparisons but to make them aware that such problems place limitations on the use of comparative data.

Control. Data gathered by external sources frequently are compiled in comparative form and used by governing boards, legislatures, and other external funding sources in decisions directly impacting the resources, activities, and missions of the individual institution. As a result, gaining and maintaining control over the comparison is critical to the individual institution, its image, and its ability to fulfill its mission. However, administrators frequently either do not or cannot gain this control. The less control the institution's administrators have over the comparison once the data leaves the institution, the higher the risk to the institution.

Frequently the problem is simply that the institution's administrators do not recognize either the importance of or the opportunity for gaining control of the comparison. Inundated by requests for data and desiring to be helpful, administrators often fail to consider how the data will be used once it leaves the institution. Further, they often fail to qualify their responses or refuse to respond to the request.

More often, however, individual administrators have little opportunity for control over the form or the use of comparisons. They are thus forced to provide on demand data that are then compiled and compared within the classification schema of the external agency or individual requesting the data.

Owing to this lack of control over the form and use of external comparisons, the college or university administrator's motivation for using peer comparisons is often defensive. In the multitude of comparisons produced over the past few years, few institutions or departments have escaped an inappropriate or even damaging peer comparison. As a result, administrators are often forced into a position of using comparative data to develop what they deem to be more sound alternative comparisons. Many administrators learn the hard way that it is necessary to preempt potentially damaging peer comparisons by framing requests and proposals in terms of peer comparisons of their own choosing.

Proliferation of Peers. Closely related to the problem of control over external comparisons is the issue of who or what controls the selection of peers and their use within the college or university's internal decision-making process. Frequently, the institution's inability to exert control over external comparisons is a reflection of a lack of internal cohesiveness in the selection and use of peer comparisons. Peers are selected on a unit-by-unit, or even an issue-by-issue, basis, which often results in a chaotic proliferation of peers within the individual institution.

Unit-by-Unit Peers. As the use of peer institution comparisons increases on many campuses, peer groups often proliferate. It is evident to many administrators and faculty that their administrative unit or academic department has its own peer group separate from the peers of other departments or the institution as a whole. Although two or more institutions may be similar on broad institutional measures, the chemistry departments of each, for example, may vary significantly in size, resources, programs, curricula, reputation, and a variety of other dimensions. In the opinion of many departmental faculty and administrators, comparison of their departments to possibly very different counterparts at other institutions provides no suitable model or viable measure for assessing performance. These administrators often select as peers departments at other institutions that are either similar to their own on one or two dimensions or a notch above.

The obvious problem with this unit-by-unit approach to choosing peers is that it creates within the institution a confusing array of peer groups, no two of which are alike. Further, this unit-by-unit peer approach ignores the broad concept of environment and its impact on the individual department or unit within the institution. Although the selection of institution-level peers is almost always conducted with the consideration of some environmental measures, such as region, control, and funding, most unit-by-unit peer selections are not so conducted. Yet, environment is as crucial a consideration at the departmental level as at the institutional level in determining both the opportunities and constraints within which the unit must operate.

For example, let us say that the physics departments at institution A and institution B wish to execute similar programs to serve similar numbers of students. However, institution A is a private institution with 12,000 students, and institution B is a large public university with 30,000 students. Further, institution A has a strong science and math core requirement for undergraduates, while requirements at institution B differ with each program. Within these different environments, it may be easier for institution A than institution B to garner the resources necessary to implement the program. Further, given the different environmental parameters of each institution, the program may be appropriate for A but not for B, regardless of its surface merits for institution B.

Issue-by-Issue Peers. In addition to selecting different peer groups for separate units, many college and university administrators choose different peer comparison groups that are specific to certain issue. For example, these administrators may use one peer group for analysis of a particular academic program, another for faculty salary comparison, and still another as a model for a specific administrative operation. Further, this selection of peer groups to fit specific issues is not confined to broad institutionwide issues but often extends to all levels of the college or university organization. The result is a further proliferation of peer groups that are selected on the basis of a wide variety of criteria, which are often unstated and frequently arbitrary.

In addition, the use of different peer groups for specific issues often presents political problems for the institution. The issue-by-issue approach to peer comparison frequently undermines the credibility of peer comparisons, particularly in the estimation of outside observers and decision makers. A public institution that bases its resource allocation requests on several different peer institution groups is likely to appear to its external audience as attempting, in an unsophisticated fashion, to "stack the deck."

Underlying the problems of internal chaos and external lack of credibility inherent in the issue-by-issue approach to peer selection is the broader issue of the a priori validity of the approach itself. At the heart of the issue are the yet-unresolved questions of the definition of the term *peer* and the purpose of peer comparisons. Much of what are called peer comparisons are often comparisons among competitors, institutions in the same jurisdictional or organizational grouping (such as athletic conferences), or aspiration models (Brinkman and Krakower, 1983). Other comparisons are chosen to justify and defend past actions and even, at times, to cover past management errors.

What is and is not a valid peer comparison has not yet been clearly defined. Practically, part of the reason for this ambiguity may lie in the fine line between what works and what does not work—what garners more resources and what does not. Yet, at some point, the issue-by-issue approach to peer comparison becomes unproductive for the institution and its individual units. Either the proliferation of peer groups within the institution becomes unwieldy or the external credibility of the comparisons begins to diminish appreciably. It is at this point that the institution and its decision makers search for a more coordinated and powerful approach to the selection and use of peer comparisons.

Several institutions and systems have dealt with the proliferation of peers by mandating that a specified institutional set of peers be used by all departments and for most issues. However, this top-down approach frequently is not broad enough to include an array of selection criteria that incorporates different department and issue considerations, particularly academic factors. What is needed is a framework for determining peers and peer comparisons that includes considerations critical to all participants, including the board, administration, and departments. Planning provides this framework.

Peers and the Planning Process

Many of the problems administrators encounter in using peer comparisons result from the inappropriate and tardy placement of the comparison in the institutional decision-making process. Frequently, the peer comparison is introduced at the end of the process as an accountability measure that is unrelated to the goals and objectives of the institution and the departments. When presented at this point, a peer comparison becomes a justification or defense. When used by a legislator, such a comparison is often a tool for reducing the college or university's allocations, staff, or programs. When peer comparisons are introduced late in the institutional decision-making process, it should be no surprise that most users grab the peer group that most fits their purposes.

The positive power of peer comparisons can be unleashed by incorporating and using the comparison group throughout the institutional planning process. In the initial stages, comparisons provide indexes of the college or university's current position. Key factors are then identified and provide a cohesive base for developing and implementing strategic plans.

Linking peer institution comparisons to institutional planning in the initial stages of the planning process also introduces parameters to the goal setting and modeling that is conducted at each level of the college or university's organizational structure. Figure 1 illustrates the institutional planning process and the role of peer comparisons incorporated throughout the process.

In the initial stage, the board, central administration, and departments typically approach the planning process with goals and models (or peers). Some of these goals and models overlap among groups, others conflict. The process of determining institutional and departmental peers and models early in the planning process is the vehicle for exposing and instigating discussion of these contradictory goals. The result of this discussion is to define institutional goals and peers that incorporate elements considered crucial by members of the board, administration, and departments. As departmental plans are then formulated and integrated into the institutional plan, department-level models are identified within the context of a range of agreed-on institutional peers.

One of the strongest arguments for using peer institution comparisons early in planning lies in the identification of differences. Through comparisons, administrators can view the range of differences among institutions and identify their own institution's strengths and weaknesses. Against this background, weaknesses can be targeted for improvement, and strengths for enhancement. Both elements then become key components in the development of the institution's strategic plan.

Environment and history provide the context for the development and implementation of a strategic plan. Peers provide viable models only if they operate in environments that have similar constraints and comparable developmental paths or historical trajectories. However, outside the planning process, both elements are often ignored in the random selection of peers by governing boards, central administration, and individual departments.

Consideration of environmental and developmental factors in the initial planning stages further acts as a catalyst for the melding of different goals and peers into a set of university peers and goals. Subsequent selection of department peers from among this broad group ensures some comparability of environment between the individual department and its models.

Figure 1. Peers and the Planning Cycle

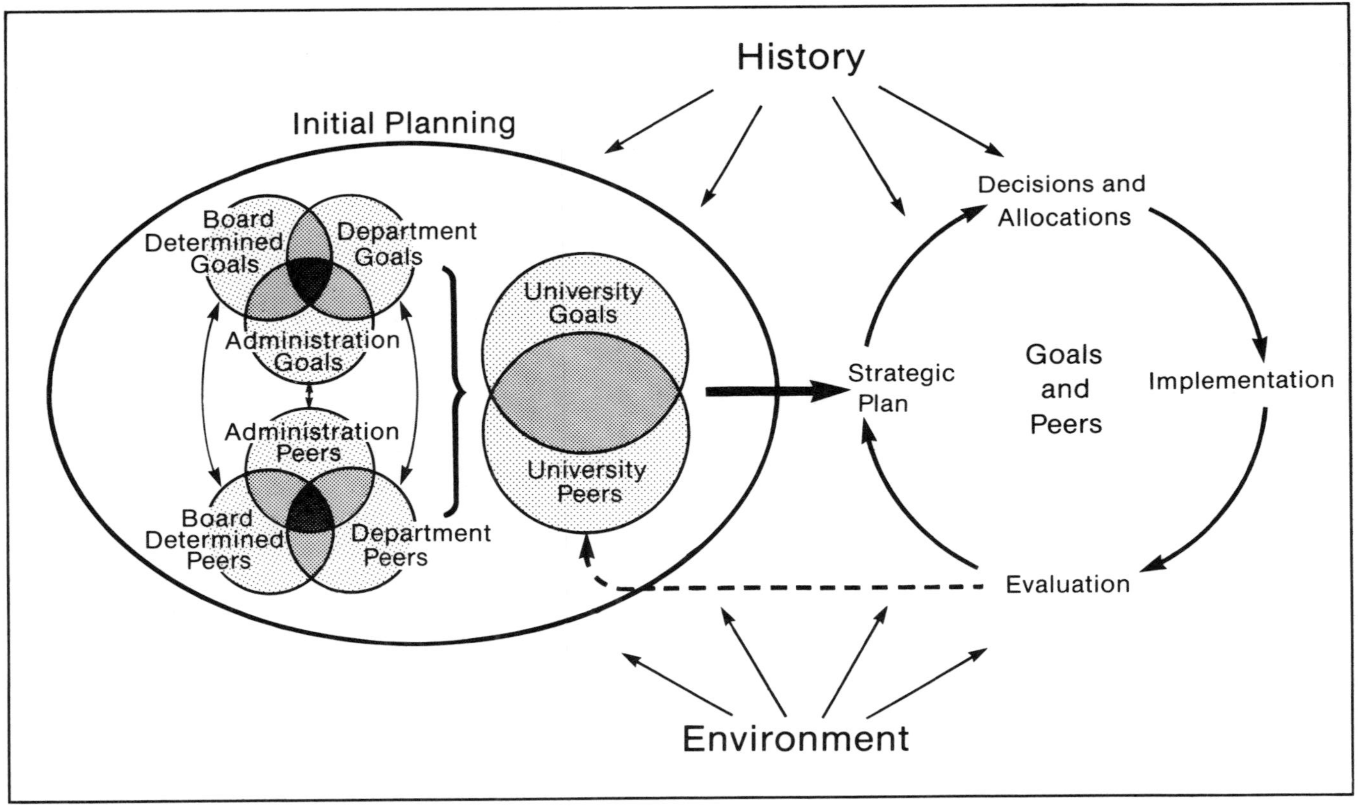

The Strategic Planning Cycle

By relating peer institution comparisons to planning, college and university administrators ensure that more appropriate peer comparisons are used at important points throughout the planning process. In an iterative, circular planning process, comparisons provide a basis for determining strategic goals. These goals, together with examples from peer institutions, form the basis for subsequent decisions and allocations. Examples from peers also provide models for the implementation stage of the planning cycle. Finally, comparisons with peers provide measures of both external and internal progress of the plan, which provides feedback for modifying the initial goals and strategic plans.

Advantages

Incorporating the selection and use of peer comparisons throughout the planning cycle further resolves a number of common problems with peer comparisons, as follows:

1. *Diversity.* Viewed against a backdrop of similar institutions, a college or university's unique characteristics are highlighted, allowing both weaknesses and strengths to be targeted in the strategic plan. Further, in the process of considering the environments and histories of peers, unique markets and niches may be identified more clearly and incorporated early into the goals of the plan.

2. *Validity.* Incorporating peer comparisons into the planning cycle does much to enhance the validity of the institution's many uses of peer comparisons. Further, it may operate to diminish the potential threat posed by incomparable data. Development of a single, stable set of peers focuses attention on a much smaller group of institutions and the problems of comparing data within that set. The result often is the establishment of mutually beneficial data exchanges across the small group of institutions with careful attention to correcting problems of comparison across the group. While all data comparison problems will not be alleviated, they will, at least, be identified clearly, thus improving the decisions made based on the comparisons.

3. *Control.* A key benefit of incorporating peers throughout the planning process is that it provides the institution and its administrators and faculty with control over comparisons. Consideration of comparisons and identification of peers early in the planning process removes the pressure often associated with selecting peers for specific decisions. Further, placing peer selection early in the planning cycle adds an element of preparedness, a key advantage for decision makers at all levels of the institution. Selection of peers at the front end gives administrators and faculty an edge in dealing with external requests for data and a sound defense against someone else's ad hoc "peer" comparison.

4. *Proliferation of Peers.* An institutionwide comparison group selected within the planning cycle provides administrators at all levels with a backdrop against which to model, make allocation decisions, and measure progress toward both institutional and departmental goals. One advantage of the broad institutional comparison group selected during initial planning is that it gives subunits parameters to guide their individual comparison group selection. Thus, overall university planning guides the subsequent selection and use of peer subgroups at all levels and on all issues. In this way, crucial environmental factors are de facto variables in the selection of peers by units and departments.

Framing the selection of peers within the context of the planning cycle does much to alleviate the common problems associated with peer comparisons in institutional decision making. Diversity is highlighted, peer selection rationalized and objectified, control achieved, and the proliferation of different peer groups eliminated. Further, the institution gains the opportunity to work with its peers to eliminate problems of data incomparability, which raises the validity of the comparisons even further. In addition, including peer comparisons from the initial stages of planning adds much to the planning process. Comparisons provide a more rational and cohesive context for all stages of the institutional planning cycle.

However, incorporating peer comparisons in the planning cycle is only an incremental step toward dealing with more substantive issues associated with the selection and use of peer comparisons. Theory has not caught up with practical application. As a result, part of the answer lies outside the purview of administrators and is the responsibility of higher education researchers.

A Broader Perspective

Problems with comparisons are not unique to the field of higher education. Today, the literature in comparative political science, history, and sociology is rich with discussions of both the methodological and theoretical issues associated with use of comparisons. Questions of how to establish stable and viable data categories, what analysis methods are best applied to comparisons (Frederickson, 1980; Mandelbaum, 1980), and whether or not comparative analysis is more valid for macro- or micro-analyses dominate much of the discussion in these fields (see Vallier, 1971).

Comparative analysis is a relatively new and ill-defined methodology that arises primarily out of the proliferation of computer-generated, quantitative data. As data and the means for restructuring data became more sophisticated, comparisons resulted. However, theory and guidelines on the use of the methodology have lagged behind application.

Despite its problems and lack of maturity as a defined methodology, comparative analysis has the potential to be a powerful operational and theoretical tool in higher education. Organizational comparison across environments and time allows for the identification of key variables and the determination of the relationships, or static sets, of these variables that can develop into themes, laws, and universals. As sociologist David Apter (1971) notes: "What a general comparative theory ought to contain is a set of formal and logical categories in the form of statements of relationships in which the variation of any one variable leads to the 'regulated' alteration in the others" (p. 9). Further, the comparative analysis process can direct attention to key theoretical constructs that are often not considered in other forms of organizational analysis.

In higher education the relationships between key institutional variables, such as quality and funding and size and needs, are unknown. Theoretical constructs that are important in the development and operation of colleges and universities have not been identified. For example, little is known about the influence of history and of the developmental stages of institutions on constraining response to change.

The strength of the comparative analysis method lies in its potential for producing information, theories, and models about change. This is what many college and university administrators are seeking when they use peer comparisons. Underlying the use of peer comparisons in the planning processes of individual colleges and universities and their departments is the need to understand the institution and move it further into the future.

However, research that uses comparative analysis is still at a very basic stage in higher education. Key institutional variables and their relationships across institutions and time have yet to be discovered. Models and theories to direct planning and the management of change in colleges and universities are still in the developmental stage.

Owing to these theoretical limitations, college or university administrators must understand the limitations of peer institution comparisons and the often unstated assumptions that underlie their use. Until research can provide more answers and direction for college or university planning, administrators must continue to rely on their own reasoned judgments for guidance in using peer comparisons. Incorporating peer comparisons into the entire fabric of the institutional planning process is a viable incremental step in increasing the power of the comparison as a critical tool in the management of change.

References

Apter, D. E. "Comparative Studies: A Review with Some Projections." In I. Vallier (ed.), *Comparative Methods in Sociology*. Berkeley: University of California Press, 1971.
Birnbaum, R. *Maintaining Diversity in Higher Education*. San Francisco: Jossey-Bass, 1983.

Brinkman, P., and Krakower, J. *Comparative Data for Administrators in Higher Education.* Boulder, Colo.: National Center for Higher Education Management Systems, 1983.

Brubacher, J. S., and Rudy, W. *Higher Education in Transition.* New York: Harper & Row, 1976.

Frederickson, G. M. "Comparative History." In M. Kammen (ed.), *The Past Before Us: Contemporary Historical Writing in the United States.* Ithaca, N.Y.: Cornell University Press, 1980.

Harris, A. H. "The Comparability Question: Potential Uses and Misuses of Data." Paper presented at the Association for Institutional Research, Vancouver, British Columbia, May 1973.

Hyatt, J. A. "Using National Financial Data for Comparative Analysis." In C. Frances (ed.), *Successful Responses to Financial Difficulty.* New Directions for Higher Education, no. 38. San Francisco: Jossey-Bass, 1982.

Hyatt, J. A., and Thompson, R. K. "State and Institutional Comparative Analyses Using HEGIS Finance Data: A Review." *Business Officer,* 1980, *13* (12), 20–24.

Jencks, C., and Reisman, D. *The Academic Revolution.* Chicago: University of Chicago Press, 1977.

Lingenfelter, P. E. "The Uses and Abuses of Interstate Comparisons of Higher Education Funding." *Business Officer,* 1983, *17* (3), 14–16.

Mandelbaum, M. "Some Forms and Uses of Comparative History." *American Studies International,* 1980, *18* (12), 19–34.

Newman, F. *Report on Higher Education.* Washington, D.C.: U.S. Department of Health, Education, and Welfare, 1971.

Southern Association of Colleges and Schools, Commission on Colleges. *The Criteria for Accreditation.* Section III. Atlanta, Ga.: Southern Colleges and Schools, Commission on Colleges, 1984.

Vallier, I. (ed.). *Comparative Methods in Sociology.* Berkeley: University of California Press, 1971.

Meredith A. Whiteley is senior research analyst for university planning and analysis, Arizona State University.

Frances K. Stage is assistant professor, educational leadership and policy studies, Indiana University.

The importance of interinstitutional comparisons at the state and system level is described, and problems to be addressed and recommended strategies are discussed.

Interinstitutional Analysis at the System and State Level

Marilyn McCoy

Higher education, like the nonprofit sector, generally relies on comparative measures to assess relative levels of need, activity, resource utilization, and performance. Two primary standards of measurement are used. One is an assessment of how a unit is faring over time. Year-to-year changes are tracked as are changes over longer periods, and incremental and decremental shifts are carefully monitored. The second major standard used is interunit comparisons. Departmental comparisons, institutional comparisons, and comparisons at the state level are used in an effort to delineate standards of appropriate treatment and achievement. At the state and system level interinstitutional comparisons provide an important metric for determining relative levels of support, institutional needs, productivity, and performance. Such comparisons provide perspectives about conditions and the operation of one unit or group of units in relation to those of similar institutions. Although interinstitutional comparisons can be made among campuses within a state, efforts to compare more similar institutions often require data about campuses in other states. This is particularly true for universities and specialized institutions such as health centers, since in many states there are only one or two such institutions.

P. T. Brinkman (ed.). *Conducting Interinstitutional Comparisons.*
New Directions for Institutional Research, no. 53. San Francisco: Jossey-Bass, Spring 1987.

Motivations for Comparisons

One of the principal values of comparative analysis is that it permits a fresh examination of current conditions to determine whether they are appropriate, given patterns at similar institutions; this analysis provides the closest approximation of standards. Such a review can lead to quite different conclusions than will incremental or decremental approaches that look at changes over time. Comparative analysis is also a useful means for identifying differential needs among a group of institutions, whereas incremental or decremental approaches tend to foster across-the-board decision making. By providing an explicit basis for determining different needs, comparisons can provide a means for differential decision making while maintaining fairness in addressing the varying needs of institutions within a system or state.

Before describing some of the principal uses of interinstitutional comparisons made by boards at the state and system level (as well as the problems and possibilities associated with such analysis), the structure and roles of these boards are explored.

Features of State and System Boards

Higher education state or system boards are present in all states in the United States. As Millard (1980, p. 67) indicates these "boards vary considerably from state to state in the number of institutions under their purview, in their powers in relation to institutions, and in the scope or applicability of their responsibilities." A number of these differences are worth highlighting.

Governing Versus Coordinating Boards. The legal authority of governing boards for the management and operation of institutions within their area of responsibility contrasts with the more limited responsibilities of coordinating boards. Although there are variances in the area and degree of responsibility of these boards, governing boards generally have more legally vested responsibility than do coordinating boards. Both types of boards assume the natural function of relating to the state executive and legislative branches of government. Given the significant role of states in funding higher education, these boards are inherently involved, although to differing degrees, in the appropriations process in each state. Because that process necessarily raises questions about enrollment levels, program offerings, student ability levels, needed facilities, and so on, state and system boards are involved in many policy discussions with external bodies at the state level in which comparative data are useful.

In terms of the internal management and operation of institutions, there is a sharp distinction between governing and coordinating boards; the former is closely involved in campus functions and the latter is generally not as involved. This distinction carries over to the state, where self-interest is more a factor for governing boards than for coordinating boards. Thus coordinating boards are positioned in between the institutions and the legislative and executive branches. Governing boards' allegiance is clearly with the institutions they represent, although they deal extensively with the offices of state government.

Specific Functions. Beyond the governing and coordinating board delineation, there are further differences in boards in terms of the areas of assigned responsibility, both nominally and de facto. These include differences in the boards' authority to recommend or prepare a consolidated budget; to approve expenditures; to determine tuition and financial aid; to alter institutional missions, to open and close institutions; to review, approve, and discontinue academic programs; to construct facilities; and to set enrollment levels and admissions standards, to cite some of the major areas of state and system decision making related to higher education. These differences will affect the range of interinstitutional comparisons that are needed by different system and state boards.

Institutional Purview. Institutional purview depends on several factors.

Number of Institutions. There are substantial differences among these boards and systems in the number of institutions within their sphere. Although state coordinating boards and some governing boards are state-wide in scope, others are not. State University of New York (SUNY), City University of New York (CUNY), and the California community college system are examples of very large systems encompassing many individual campuses. By contrast, a system such as the University of Colorado is an example of a very small board that only represents four university campuses.

Types of Institutions. There is again no uniformity in the type of institutions encompassed by these systems. Some systems are relatively homogenous, such as the University of California system with nine doctoral and research universities. Others are very heterogeneous, such as the SUNY system, with thirty-one campuses encompassing research, comprehensive, general baccalaureate, two-year academic and occupational, health professional, and other specialized professional campuses.

Control. Although most of the state and system boards have authority for public institutions only, a fair number of state coordinating boards do have some scope of interaction with independent institutions, for example, for financial aid, capitation support, facilities, or research in support of economic development.

The foregoing review of differences among state and system boards in scope, authority, and function provides a basis for a few observations that relate to interinstitutional comparisons at the state and system level.

Governing boards will inherently have greater need and appetite for a wider range of interinstitutional comparisons than will coordinating boards, which have more limited authority and responsibility.

As the number of institutions within a system or state board increases, the need to develop systematic means of coordination and management becomes more critical. At the same time the technical requirements of identifying appropriate peer groups and effective interinstitutional analysis sensitive to the significant differences in these institutions increases.

The more similar the mission of the institutions within a single board or system, the easier it should be to identify appropriate peer groups and methods of analysis. The university system in California is a case in point. At the other extreme would be the SUNY system, which represents institutions of almost every category and requires an extensive national base of information and data sharing.

Useful Applications

Financial comparisons are the most prevalent area of interinstitutional comparisons at the state and system level. Comparisons of faculty salaries, revenue and expenditure per student, departmental costs, and tuition levels are regularly made both in system offices and by state boards. Given the key role of these groups in the appropriations and budgeting process, the need for and applicability of such comparisons is easily understood. Some of these comparisons are used to derive standards that are then embedded in budget formulas during appropriations in the state or system.

Beyond the financial area the uses of interinstitutional comparisons are more limited, variable, and specific to individual situations. Stated differently, there is a wide range of potential comparisons that could be made employing existing data sources that are not in popular use in most system and state board offices. The following listing details some of the areas where interinstitutional comparisons are made and, more important, could be made more extensively:

1. Academic Programs
   a. Degrees granted by field
   b. Program quality ratings
   c. Tenure rates
   d. Research support
   e. Comparisons of library holdings
   f. Student/faculty ratios
2. Students
   a. Profiles of student financial aid
   b. Origins of students by state
   c. Student test scores
   d. Enrollment trends by race, sex, and student level

3. Facilities
   a. Capacity and usage
   b. Condition
4. Development
   a. Levels of giving
   b. Support per alumni

Data in these areas could provide useful input to planning efforts, specific program decision making, facilities support, and so on. What is apparent is that despite improvements in data availability and technological capacity to process data, interinstitutional comparisons are less prevalent and more narrowly focused than one might expect.

Other Issues

The preceding sections have, for interinstitutional comparisons, highlighted a number of important difficulties that are inherent in the structure of systems and boards. Although these difficulties vary in degree, they are due to the diversity of institutions, the number of institutions addressed, and the range of responsibilities and authority represented. There are other factors that affect interinstitutional comparisons at the system and state level. These factors follow.

Multiplicity of Staff. In many states, the legislature and executive offices have been developing independent staffs specializing in higher education. In part these staff reflect the increasing technical complexity of issues facing state government. Their presence can provide an informed resource at each stage of the state policy process. They can also create a competing base for information about higher education. Building support for interinstitutional comparisons within these staffs is an important ingredient to successful comparisons.

Conflicts at the State Level. The willingness to support cooperative efforts across the executive and legislative branches can have an important impact on the successful development of comparative analyses. Developing agreement on comparison groups and methods of analysis and presentation is an important task that must be confronted by the executive and legislative bodies. Although there are variations in the relative power of these branches, their cooperation is important in efforts to unify communication about higher education.

Audience Receptivity. The use of interinstitutional comparisons presupposes a receptivity to analytical and rational input to public policy discussions. Depending on the results of such comparisons, different audiences may vary in their willingness to accept findings that contradict their prior opinions or that present different political agendas, such as the need for greater funding, criticism of student access rates or admissions, and so forth. Sensitivity to these concerns and a willingness to pursue the educational component associated with using comparative data are important.

Changing Issues. Because the process of making interinstitutional comparisons can be so complex, involving developing peer groups, devising acceptable methods of analysis, collecting data, analyzing the information, and presenting it to different audiences, it is important to develop an agenda of key topics to analyze. These issues should preferably be topics of recurring interest. Owing to the variety of issues that can arise at the state and system level, the process of agenda-setting is clearly challenging.

Statistical Complexities. Some of the statistical and analytical tasks associated with effective interinstitutional comparisons can be complex. For example, the methodology used for selecting peer groups can be elaborate. Maintaining that rigor and at the same time reducing the black-box character of this work can be difficult. For one-time analyses this is particularly troublesome. For those analyses that become part of the repertoire of state and board discussions, repeated exposure will reduce these difficulties.

Comparability of Data. The development of interinstitutional comparisons usually involves the use of data from institutions in different states and at times from multiple sources as well. Given the different populations that may be covered and variances in definitions, the ability to profile all institutions within a system or state may be compromised.

Currency of Data. Since the desire for information is generally set within the context of current decision making, the timeliness of data is an important issue. Data that are available are generally somewhat late, usually by at least one year. For example, one major national source of higher education institutional data, Higher Education General Information Surveys (HEGIS), maintained by the Center for Statistics, usually lags two to three years behind for computerized files and even longer for detailed published reports.

The development of personal networks of technical staffs in states and institutions is important and can help in obtaining more current data. For example, the public research universities have established a network (the AAU Data Exchange) and share data on a regular basis. In addition, these groups have provided a source of timely information for special purpose phone surveys, such as information about planned tuition and faculty salaries or expected changes in state appropriations.

Sources of Data. As soon as a need for information is defined, the make or buy question must be confronted. Although data collected by the state or system can be designed to more closely address the specific issues at hand and to be more timely, such data are likely to represent lower response rates and lesser comparability and require greater costs to obtain and analyze than do long-standing data collection or published studies by major recognized groups.

Groupings of Institutions. As previously noted, in large systems it is very difficult to formulate informed policy on an institution-by-institution basis; some analytical context is usually needed. As a starting point it is generally helpful to use broad aggregations of institutions to develop a profile. Simple delineations such as university, four-year, and two-year institutions are frequently used. A more detailed classification, such as a Carnegie classification or that developed by NCHEMS, may be even more helpful. A more tailored approach is to develop a system of peer institutions that reflects the specific characteristics of each institution. This approach is highly recommended but can be somewhat complex to develop. (Strategies for identifying peer groups were commented on previously.)

Many state systems—such as university systems, community college boards, state college systems, and so forth—developed with an institutional grouping as part of their governing structure. In some cases these groupings include similar institutions. In other states these groupings can represent quite different schools. In the latter cases an alternative categorization is technically preferable but may encounter political resistance from those accustomed to existing governing structures.

Desire for Determinacy. It is a natural tendency in addressing policy issues to want to simplify the issue at hand. Analyses however are seldom so clear-cut, and there are usually important qualifying factors that must be considered. The desire for simple solutions is particularly prevalent in governmental policy forums owing to the multiplicity of issues facing these bodies. Addressing this simplicity-complexity dilemma is one of the important tasks that must be faced in interinstitutional analysis.

Cost of Comparative Data. There are important variations in what one might spend to obtain interinstitutional data. At the low end is the purchase of completed published analyses, such as those provided by various governmental agencies, private research groups, higher education consortiums, and individual researchers. At the high end is the collecting and analyzing of extensive data sets of one's own design or the commissioning of someone else to do this. Between these extremes is the joining of various data exchange groups to obtain computer-based data to analyze.

Development and Use of Interinstitutional Data

Although the list of hurdles to be dealt with in obtaining and using interinstitutional data at the state and system level is sizeable, there are some general strategies that can make the process both more manageable and productive.

Attention to Process. Establishing an effective process of communication and joint effort among all parties is essential to the successful use of comparative data in these areas. Given the variety of players in the policy process, the technical complexity of developing and using interinstitutional data, the unease of many of the parties about potential agendas associated with such analyses, among other complicating factors, it is axiomatic that a participatory process is needed. For matters within a system or board, an individual campus, or a large system, representative campus members should be involved with the central staffs at each phase of development and use to ensure collective understanding if not support. For issues of a more external nature, the involvement of campuses (or selected representation for each type of school) whose data will be used as well as the state board or system staff, executive, and legislative staffs who are part of the audience for such studies should be actively involved throughout the process. Such involvement should be conducive to developing mutual understanding and education about the issue and to centralizing the information flow among multiple parties.

Setting the Agenda. As part of the process of mutual involvement, a necessary and important step should be efforts to agree on important issues that warrant interinstitutional study. Such a step is valuable for identifying priority issues and establishing a pattern of analysis that can be replicated over time. This also allows for the development of expertise in the conduct of such studies and the education of audiences about the multiple facets of these issues. It is important in this process to standardize the format of presentation as much as possible so that legislators, institutional representatives, and others become familiar with the content and appropriate applications of such analyses.

Use of Available Sources. It is both difficult and expensive to initiate new data-collection efforts. Response rates for one-time and new efforts are often not very satisfactory. Institutional and state respondents frequently face difficulties when trying to reconcile variations in questionnaire content using available in-house records. Further, delays in collecting and analyzing information often are longer than the time frame allowed for policy decisions. All of these factors underscore the value of attempting to utilize existing sources when possible. (Numerous such sources are mentioned in Chapters Two and Three.) Efforts should be made to become familiar with these avenues before initiating new collection efforts.

Multiple Levels of Aggregation. Although use of a standard taxonomy or sets of peer groups for data comparisons is desirable, use of these broad profiles should be supplemented with more disaggregated data that illuminates individual institutional differences. In part the process of interaction with campus personnel at all stages of comparative analysis helps ensure that important distinctions will be noted.

Profiles Versus Single Numbers. The purpose of interinstitutional comparisons should be to illuminate the story around an issue rather than the development of a single statistic. Owing to the complexity of most issues, one statistic seldom represents the various dimensions of the issue examined. For example, rankings of institutional expenditure levels can be misleading because they do not, by themselves, reflect the differing services that are provided, the types of students that are enrolled, and other such factors that are important to framing policies for dealing with such issues. Defining the key elements of each story and educating audiences is one of the important tasks system and state board offices can perform.

Attention to Politics. Although it is difficult to make general statements about the politics of these processes, a number of points can be proffered. The broad sharing of information to the main parties involved has been advocated. This sharing can develop support and education and also help avoid the political use of information by one party against another. In addition, as state audiences become comfortable with analyses that are replicated and publicized annually, there should be less suspicion about the political motivations for such work. Although some suspicion is inevitable, sharing important analyses should decrease this attitude. Because data comparisons are so time and labor intensive, the issues should be selected carefully and political receptivity to such work paid special attention.

Concluding Comments

Interest in interinstitutional comparisons assumes that information is valued as part of management and decision-making processes. Comparative data as distinguished from general information is useful because it inherently lends perspective about relative conditions and provides a basis for differential decision making that is fairer because the basis for differentiation is explicit. The process of developing and using comparative data is both complex and costly. Such investments are best made in support of issues that are high priority and likely to be of continuing interest. In such cases the skills of the analyst and the understanding of the audience can develop over time.

Much of the interinstitutional analysis in higher education has been in the financial area, with far less analysis in the more qualitative, less tractable areas such as educational quality and performance. But with increasing interest and national attention, analysis in these areas is likely to become more important.

Reference

Millard, R. M., "Power of State Coordinating Agencies." In P. Jedamus, M. W. Peterson, and Associates (eds.), *Improving Academic Management: A Handbook of Planning and Institutional Research.* San Francisco: Jossey-Bass, 1980.

Marilyn McCoy is vice-president for administration and planning at Northwestern University. She previously served as the planning officer for the University of Colorado system.

Can interinstitutional comparisons actually change a state's higher education budgeting? This chapter presents a case study of financial analysis and advocacy at a major state university.

University Financial Analysis Using Interinstitutional Data

*Frederick S. Lane, James S. Lawrence,
Herman Mertins, Jr.*

In November 1982 West Virginia University inaugurated a new president, E. Gordon Gee, formerly dean of its law school. Early on in his term, Gee stated that revitalization and renewal of the University was his top priority. Toward this purpose Gee initated both an internal self-study and a thorough external review of the University.

This initiative was launched in response to a recognized need for fundamental reassessment of the University's mission, capabilities, and, above all, potential. Central to the endeavor was the question of how the institution's limited resources could be best applied and new funds could be generated to deal with chronic, long-standing underfunding.

West Virginia University (WVU) is a comprehensive land-grant university established in 1867. WVU has fifteen schools and colleges, some eighteen thousand students, a main campus located in Morgantown, West Virginia, seventy miles south of Pittsburgh, three branch campuses, five off-campus graduate centers, and many statewide activities.

The comprehensive external review of WVU was headed by a four-person panel. The members were: Clark Kerr, President Emeritus of the University of California and formerly chairman of the Carnegie Commis-

P. T. Brinkman (ed.). *Conducting Interinstitutional Comparisons.*
New Directions for Institutional Research, no. 53. San Francisco: Jossey-Bass, Spring 1987.

sion on Higher Education; Alvin C. Eurich, president of the Academy for Educational Development and formerly chancellor of the State University of New York; Frederick S. Lane, chairperson of the Department of Public Administration, Bernard M. Baruch College, City University of New York; and John S. Wilson, then provost, Virginia Polytechnic Institute and State University and later president of Washington and Lee University.

The external assessment activities were supported by a grant from the Benedum Foundation, Pittsburgh (see Academy for . . . , 1984). In addition to the guiding general panel, the Benedum review process was to include forty-two of the nation's leading experts in higher education, divided into fourteen committees. Committee chairs included, for example, Victor Baldridge (enrollment management), Ernest Boyer (governance), John Goodlad (education), and E. K. Fretwell (undergraduate studies).

By spring 1983 the general panel and almost all the specialized committees visiting WVU had the same observation: West Virginia University appeared to be seriously underfunded in almost all of its areas of endeavor. This was especially emphasized by the finance committee.

But, how does a university demonstrate that it is underfunded? Most public colleges and universities currently make this argument. In April 1983 Lane proposed that a "quick and dirty" comparative analysis be attempted to document for the first time WVU's relative standing compared with peer institutions. The Benedum panel generally approved the study. Frederick Lane and James Lawrence carried out the exploratory analysis, and Herman Mertins served as the institutional liaison. The report was submitted in January 1984 (see Lane and Lawrence), 1984.

The Research Approach

The purpose of the analysis was to analyze the patterns of state budgeting and resource allocation to West Virginia University. Two basic approaches were used: (1) Funding for WVU by budget category was compared with eighteen peer institutions across the country, and (2) WVU's allocations were analyzed to determine how budget formulas used in many states (and most Southern Regional Education Board [SREB] states, of which West Virginia was one) would affect the University's funding. The study also included interviews with appropriate officials at West Virginia University, the Board of Regents, and the State Department of Finance during the summer of 1983.

To develop the set of peer institutions, a list of comparable universities was formed as follows: First, a list of all public land-grant universities with medical centers was developed. Then additional universities that were flagship universities in their state and had some health science activities although not necessarily a medical school were added to this list. Finally, three large, comprehensive nearby universities with which WVU often competes and is often compared—Pennsylvania State University, University of Pittsburgh, and Virginia Polytechnic Institute—were added to the list. Basic characteristics of these institutions were examined to confirm their comparability for the purposes of this study.

Expenditure data for eighteen institutions and WVU for 1980-1981, the most recent year then available, were collected as part of the annual Higher Education General Information Survey (HEGIS) conducted by the National Center for Education Statistics (NCES), a unit of the U.S. Department of Education, and made available with the assistance of the National Center for Higher Education Management Systems, Boulder, Colorado.

Regarding state formulas for the funding of higher education, the authors selected four states. Each is in close physical proximity to West Virginia, had similar tax capacity, and used a relatively sophisticated resource allocation formula. These states were Kentucky, Tennessee, Virginia, and Maryland. Table 1 indicates the tax capacity for these states as of 1981, the most recent year then available. All four states as well as West Virginia had a tax capacity below the fifty-state average.

In addition to the formulas used by these four states, data from actual allocations or expenditures were used when possible. In these four states special attention was paid to their university-level institutions, particularly the University of Kentucky (UK) at Lexington, University of Tennessee (UT) at Knoxville, Virginia Polytechnic Institute (VPI), and the University of Maryland (UM) at College Park. Furthermore, formulas in use in selected other states were reviewed and were occasionally referred to in the report.

When possible the budget formulas were applied to WVU data and

Table 1. 1981 Tax Capacity[1] Index for the States of Tennessee, Kentucky, West Virginia, Virginia, and Maryland

State	State Tax Capacity Index[2]
Tennessee	79
Kentucky	82
West Virginia	90
Virginia	94
Maryland	98

Source: Advisory Commission . . . , 1983).

[1] Tax capacity is a yardstick for measuring the per capita capacity of individual states to collect revenues. It includes one standard measure, individual income, but also includes twenty-five other indicators, including general and selected sales, licenses, corporate income, value of property, value of mineral production, and estates and gifts.

[2] Fifty state average = 100. For example, an index of 110 would mean 10 percent above average per capita capacity of a state to raise tax revenues; 90 would mean 10 percent below average.

comparisons made within each budget category. This was intended to help the reader decide whether a particular category was appropriately funded.

As might be expected, there were technical problems in comparing budget formulas, budgets, and institutional data across states. For example, accounting systems are not standardized across states, enrollments are reported somewhat differently, fringe benefits are included in some cases and not in others, faculty are counted in various ways, and health science complexes are budgeted in ways that frequently overlap with the main university budget.

As a result the data found in the report could not be precise to the nearest dollar. The data, however, were sufficiently valid to give an accurate picture of general patterns and major differences. The level of validity involved was reinforced by the fact that two different methodological approaches—analysis of eighteen peer institutions as well as four formulas-budget states—were used in combination.

Findings

By far the single most important conclusion of the analysis was that the instructional portion of WVU's budget was significantly poorer than those of peer institutions across the country. Further, it was much less than what it would have been if WVU were located in one of those four states with a rational formula for allocating funds to higher education institutions.

In 1980-1981 the HEGIS data showed West Virginia University with $2,682 per FTE for instruction, only 82 percent of the average university in the group of eighteen peers and the second poorest. Among nearby state universities, Virginia Polytechnic Institute had $2,885; University of Kentucky, $3,449; Penn State, $2,776; and Ohio State, $3,169.

HEGIS reported WVU's student-faculty ratio at 17.8 to 1, slightly better than the average of 20.2 to 1, although WVU compared unfavorably to 14.8 to 1 at VPI and 16.1 to 1 at UK. HEGIS data were somewhat puzzling when compared with institutional data. The fact that WVU had a somewhat better student-faculty ratio but a lower cost per student than the other institutions might reflect a low salary structure for faculty and staff and may also reflect poorer support staffing.

The HEGIS data showed WVU with $46.1 million for instruction, while the University data for 1981-1982 showed only $27.5 million. The explanation for the discrepancy is that health science center costs were included in the HEGIS data.

State Budget Formulas. The funding formulas of the states involved were applied to WVU.

Kentucky. Kentucky's funding formula for 1983-1984 was applied to WVU's enrollments found in its 1981-1982 data book. Since data were not reported separately for doctoral enrollments, it was assumed that 10 percent of graduate enrollment was at the advanced graduate level (based on the proportion of degrees granted). This was a relatively important assumption since the formulas tend to provide a high level of funding for doctoral work.

The results showed that WVU would receive much larger funding and staffing with the Kentucky formula than it had in 1981-1982, with the Kentucky formula generating $48.0 million and 1,168 FTE faculty. Then the formula adds 28 percent of the instruction figure for academic support/ instructional mission scope. This generated another $13.4 million (a figure so large that it probably includes something like experimental farms, laboratory schools, and so on).

When the WVU data was updated to 1983-1984 ($32.3 million) and the thirty-two student credit hours dropped to thirty to make them comparable, Kentucky's formula still generated many more dollars and staff than WVU actually had, possibly on the order of two hundred more faculty and at least $10 to $15 million more in funding.

Tennessee. Tennessee's 1983-1984 formula combined instruction with academic support, excluding the library. It was similar to the Kentucky formula, with four course levels plus law, and it had twenty-nine academic programs (several not applicable to universities). No student-faculty ratios were shown; the formula had dollar rates per quarter hour. The rates were significantly lower than those in Kentucky.

To apply the formula, we combined some of the Tennessee program categories into a framework like Kentucky's, applied a fringe benefit rate of 22 percent to 85 percent of the results, and multiplied the result by 1.5 to convert quarter hours to semester hours. The result was $42.7 million. Some portion of this was for the nonlibrary academic support; also, the rates were for 1983-1984, and therefore two years later than the WVU data used here, but still yielded about $6.4 million more funding than WVU had.

Tennessee's actual instructional budget for 1983-1984 had a student-faculty ratio of 18.9 to 1, slightly better than WVU's 1981-1982 ratio. In 1981-1982, Tennessee had $2,000 per FTE for instruction, a figure that rose to $2,283 in 1982-1983. Both would be higher than WVU by a significant factor, again suggesting that WVU's faculty salaries and, possibly, support staff were the major problem.

Virginia. Virginia's formula applied to WVU's 1981-1982 enrollments yielded 1,323 faculty, far more than the 967 faculty budgeted at WVU and equivalent to a 14.2 to 1 student-faculty ratio. The support staff ratio then would generate 397 positions, far more than WVU's 238.

The Virginia formula would provide WVU another $10 million in its instructional budget for positions at WVU's current salary levels. If those salaries were at the level of salaries in Virginia, even greater funding would have to be provided.

The actual formula may not work quite this well. Virginia Polytechnic Institute's budget request for 1984–1985 had an overall student-faculty ratio of 16.4 to 1, and the support positions were budgeted at 4.3 to 1 rather than 3.3 to 1.

Maryland. Maryland's formula used dollar rates per credit hour for four levels (lower and upper divisions, graduate, and graduate research) and three types of academic programs. The formula provided $183,000 as a base funding, plus the matrix, plus 37 percent of outside research funding.

The formula matrix yielded $45.7 million for 1981–1982. Adding the $183,000 and 37 percent of WVU's outside research yielded a total of $47.7 million.

The actual University of Maryland budget for 1981–1982 had a student-faculty ratio of 16.2 to 1 and a cost per FTE of $2,219, both much better than WVU's. Maryland's salaries were considerably better than WVU's.

Even if the research component was subtracted, the Maryland formula yielded far more funding than WVU received, at least $10 million.

The West Virginia Board of Regents has a student-faculty ratio model that provides for differentiations in staffing levels of instruction. Although there are problems with the formula, the most important fact is that *it is not used.*

Faculty Salaries. In one technical sense faculty salaries are not a direct formula issue, but they are an interconnected aspect of institutional expenditures. Owing to the low level of expenditures for instruction at WVU, the report also carefully analyzed the salaries of instructional staff.

WVU's salary problems are summarized in Table 2. In 1975–1976 the average salary at WVU was 91.4 percent of the average salary at the eighteen peer institutions. By 1982–1983 this had fallen to 84.6 percent, over 15 percent below the average salary at the peer institution. Table 2 also reflects data for public universities nationwide and for West Virginia's census region. The picture was extremely poor.

Where faculty salaries are extremely low, there sometimes is a tendency to inflate the rate of promotion to the upper faculty ranks to partially offset the low salary schedule. Table 3 analyzes faculty distribution by rank for WVU, the eighteen-university peer group, national and regional groups of universities. In all cases, WVU actually has a *lower* percentage of full professors and a lower percentage in the two senior ranks.

Conclusions and Recommendations. By far the largest single problem found in the analysis was that WVU's instructional budget was significantly lower than those of peer institutions across the country and in formula-funded universities in neighboring states. Full application of the formulas in operation in other states would give WVU $10 million or more than they actually had in 1983–1984. The largest increase, $15.7 million, would result from applying fully the formula from Kentucky, a state

Table 2. Average Salaries for West Virginia University and
Various Groups of Comparable Universities by Rank,
1975-1976 and 1981-1983

Academic Rank[6]	WVU	Peer Group[1]	All U.S. Public Universities[2]	South Atlantic States[5] All[3]	Public[4]
1975-1976					
Professor	21,600	24,250	24,150	24,030	na
Associate Professor	16,930	18,140	18,010	17,650	na
Assistant Professor	13,400	14,840	14,690	14,400	na
Instructor	11,210	11,870	11,510	11,400	na
All combined	16,480	(19,050)	(18,580)	(17,920)	—
Overall[7]	16,420	18,020	17,860	17,620	—
1982-1983					
Professor	31,730	39,050	38,180	39,130	38,740
Associate Professor	25,670	29,270	28,310	28,580	28,400
Assistant Professor	20,650	24,590	23,170	23,150	23,060
Instructor	16,570	18,080	17,550	18,160	17,890
All combined	25,780	(31,670)	(30,590)	(30,320)	(29,960)
Overall[7]	25,780	30,630	29,580	30,020	29,790
WVU 1975-1976 Average Salaries as Percentage of Those in Various Groups Above					
Professor		89.1	89.4	89.9	—
Associate Professor		93.3	94.0	95.9	—
Assistant Professor		90.3	91.2	93.1	—
Instructor		94.4	97.4	98.3	—
Overall		91.4	92.3	93.7	—
WVU 1982-1983 Average Salaries as Percentage of Those in Various Groups Above					
Professor		81.3	83.1	81.1	81.9
Associate Professor		87.7	90.7	89.8	90.4
Assistant Professor		84.0	89.1	89.2	89.5
Instructor		91.6	94.4	91.2	92.6
Overall		84.6	87.9	86.8	87.4

Source: Prepared by Maryse Eymonerie Associates, McLean, Va., at the authors' request. Based on data obtained from the National Center for Education Statistics (NCES Form 2300-3), U.S. Department of Education.
[1] Includes University of Arizona, University of Kentucky, Michigan State University, University of Missouri, University of Hawaii, University of Nevada, Ohio State University, University of Florida, University of Wisconsin, University of Minnesota, Texas A & M University, University of California at Davis, Pennsylvania State University, University of Georgia, University of Pittsburg, Louisiana State University, Virginia Polytechnic Institute, and University of Vermont. Data on standard academic year basis.

Table 2. *(continued)*

[2] Includes all public category I universities in the nation (universities awarding at least thirty doctorates per year); N = 105

[3] N = 24

[4] N = 15

[5] States include: Delaware, Maryland, District of Columbia, Virginia, North Carolina, South Carolina, Georgia, and Florida (as well as West Virginia).

[6] The rank of lecturer was excluded from this table

[7] Because the percentage of faculty within ranks is somewhat different for WVU than for other groups, we used a Paasche index to compute the overall averages. (The distribution of faculty members at WVU was used as the weight.)

Table 3. Percentage Distribution within Ranks for WVU and Various Groups of Comparable Universities, 1982-1983

Academic Rank	WVU	Peer Group	All U.S. Public Universities	South Atlantic States All	South Atlantic States Public
Professor	33.8	42.0	40.6	35.8	34.6
Associate Professor	31.8	28.4	29.9	31.7	32.5
Assistant Professor	29.1	24.6	25.0	27.2	27.6
Instructor	5.2	5.0	4.5	5.4	5.3
All	99.9[1]	100.0	100.0	100.0	100.0

Source: See Table 2.

[1] Does not add to 100 due to rounding.

with a 1981 tax capacity lower than West Virginia's. Even at the level of 84 percent of the formula funded at the University of Kentucky in that year, the increase would have been $13.2 million. Although it is difficult to separate the various components, it seemed clear that

1. WVU's salaries were far too low compared to peer institutions at all ranks, and WVU's relative position had declined in recent years.

2. The WVU student-faculty ratios were inadequate, and as many as 100 additional faculty might have been justifiable, even using a relatively conservative formula.

3. Instructional support staffing also seemed inadequate. A significant increase could have been justified here.

The report also looked at other components of the educational and general (E&G) budget. Although the WVU library budget seemed more than adequate for a well-established library, the collection size was inadequate, and additional funds were needed to permit the library to gain appropriate size in volumes and to increase its periodical subscriptions.

Student services staffing at WVU may have been somewhat inadequate, and increases could be justified in relation to the formulas and actual experience in other states.

In other budget categories there was insufficient evidence to draw any firm conclusions. The salary issue, of course, most likely played a role in all of the categories.

Some budget categories are difficult to specify in formula terms. This requires in-depth and joint analysis of the nature of WVU's mission and condition by state officials and the Regents as well as by University administrators.

The most important conclusion and recommendation made related to the need for a logical and consistent approach to allocating state funds to institutions of higher education in West Virginia. The approach favored is founded on appropriate institutional peer comparisons throughout the system. Formula-funded institutional allocations in West Virginia would greatly help focus on the character and missions of its various colleges and universities. We could not emphasize enough the importance that the Regents, state executive and legislative branch officials, and institutional representatives begin to develop models for resource allocation that are appropriate and equitable to the various kinds of institutions in the state.

WVU is the state's only comprehensive, research university and also its land-grant institution. The Regents' student-faculty ratio model, had it been used, would have been fairer than the nonformula-based approach used in addressing WVU's instructional problems. It is quite apparent that if West Virginia University were located in any of the four nearby formula-funded states analyzed in this study, its instructional budget would improve significantly. West Virginia needed to respond to these issues in its decision making for higher education.

Reactions

Copies of the technical report prepared by Lane and Lawrence were available in the winter of 1984. This included some staff members of the State Board of Regents. The report was viewed as an interesting intellectual exercise, but essentially there was no reaction, even to the implied criticism. Later, when the University incorporated some of the analysis and findings in its annual budget request, there was still no reaction. At least at first the analytical strategy had failed.

But the Benedum review panel was much more impressed with the findings of the financial analysis and included them among its principal findings when their final report was released (with great fanfare) in fall 1984. Stung by the criticism of such an important group of outsiders, this time the chancellor responded—not with more dollars but with an attempt to discredit the logic of the financial analysis.

Although many arguments were made publicly by the chancellor of the state system, three were paramount. First, it was claimed that WVU already received favorable treatment. It was pointed out that WVU received 43 percent of the Regents' allocation to higher education even though

WVU had less than 30 percent of the state's students attending public institutions.

Second, the usefulness of a formula was denied, the argument being that a formula would not help raise more money for higher education. The alternative, it was stressed, was to take funds away from other colleges and universities in the state. Both of these criticisms ignored any benefits, indeed the considerable benefits, that can be derived from interinstitutional comparisons of all categories of institutions.

Over the years WVU received a nearly fixed percentage amount from the Regents, regardless of the size of increase in appropriations granted by the legislature, program or enrollment changes, or other factors. Excluding line items and the medical center, the Regents budgeted no more than 43.76 percent of its funds and no less than 43.15 percent of its funds to West Virginia University in the seven-year period from 1977–1978 to 1983–1984.

The chancellor's staff also began homework of their own. They faulted the technical analysis regarding what WVU might have received in any of the four nearby formula-drive states. Even though WVU would have gained by using any of the four states' formulas, none of the states fully funded their formulas the following year.

The Benedum report criticized the Regents and its staff for overregulation and on other matters and this apparently affected the Regents' response to the financial recommendations. Moreover, the Regents were generally having a difficult time with the state legislature, and their very existence was scheduled for review under the state's "sunset" legislation. All these factors complicated the Regents' reactions.

At the same time many in the legislature and the media (see "WVU Funding," 1984) seemed to have little difficulty understanding the arguments and the positive contribution that peer analysis can make in clarifying some of the differences.

Eventually, President Gee, in part frustrated by the state's reluctance to better fund WVU, left to take a position as president of the University of Colorado. Another governor was elected in West Virginia and employed his budgetary and other powers differently from the previous administration. The resignation of the chancellor followed, and the legislature postponed the "sunset" review of the Regents until 1988 to increase the scrutiny and "keep the heat on." The governor took a different approach, calling for the abolition of the Regents and their replacement by a three-person commission. This proposal was not enacted, but it certainly directed attention to higher education problems in the state and helped lead to the formation of the Higher Education Study Commission, which is slated to make recommendations to the 1987 legislature.

Although the comparative analysis documented what many at WVU and in the state's higher education establishment already knew and also changed the thinking of some, no new funds were made available to WVU as a result of the study.

Technical Problems in Interstate and Interinstitutional Analysis

The American federal system has many advantages, but ease of comparison among the states is not one of them. Comparisons among higher education institutions, which pride themselves on their autonomy, are further complicated, sometimes even within the same state.

The results of interinstitutional comparisons, therefore, cannot be viewed as absolute truths. Rather, they become guidelines for more detailed state or local reviews that take into account both the technical problems and local policies and concerns. For such comparisons it is essential that technical problems are clarified so that state or local officials can better carry out their review functions.

Peer Institutions. If one is to make formulaic or budgeting comparisons, comparable units, or peers, must be selected. Program comparability is particularly crucial, but size, location, and other factors may also need to be considered. Selection of such peers is the first technical issue that must be solved.

In the West Virginia project, two different, complementary approaches were applied. First, the state is surrounded by somewhat similar states with reasonably similar universities. That is, Kentucky, Tennessee, Virginia, and Maryland all adjoin West Virginia, share many of the characteristics of West Virginia, and make up a somewhat natural basis of comparison that would be recognized by public officials. Each state also has a major university center sharing some of the characteristics of West Virginia University. Finally, each of the comparison states applies budget formulas to its universities.

This somewhat subjective but natural geographic group of peers was supplemented in the study by the more systematic peer group developed using the federal HEGIS data. Higher education institutions report annually on expenditures, revenues, enrollments, library holdings, and other factors, following a standard reporting format, which should make interstate and interinstitutional comparisons more straightforward. Actual reporting practices and local decisions concerning classification of expenditures have been and remain problematic. But, even so, the data bases offer more promise of uniformity than other sources. The extensive data allow one to apply any number of criteria to developing peers. In this case, size of enrollment, full-time versus part-time enrollments, proportion of doctoral enrollments, and existence of a medical school were among the factors considered, but others could have easily been used.

Each of the approaches used to develop peers in the West Virginia study raised technical problems. In the geographic approach, both Maryland and Virginia and the respective universities in those states differ in many important respects from West Virginia. The University of Maryland is far larger and more complex than West Virginia University. Moreover, Maryland is a wealthier state than West Virginia and hence more able to fund its university through larger tax capacity.

The more sophisticated approach using HEGIS data also has its problems. Although a university in Wyoming, for example, might appear comparable to one in West Virginia, based on various numerical indicators, it is unlikely that public or university officials in either state would give much weight to such a comparison because of the vast geographic separation and differing traditions, priorities, and fiscal abilities. The more the comparison criteria are refined, the more likely it is that such "odd couples" will result if the number of such institutions is small in the first place.

These two approaches used together, to the extent that the data are available, seem to provide a reasonable balance that provides both a commonsense appeal and a technically valid basis for comparisons. There are factors that transcend such data, however; in particular, a state's history and the priority it accords a specific function at a given point in time must be considered. If a state's prison system has deteriorated, for example, higher education may have less funds budgeted for a time.

Data Comparability. Once the peers are selected, one can begin to develop and analyze comparative data (assuming these are available). Any number of problems can then arise. Despite valiant efforts, categories of expenditures and revenues are not clearly uniform among states and institutions. As noted earlier, in the actual reporting an expense might be considered part of an instructional budget for one institution and be listed under a student services or administrative budget category for another. It often is very difficult for the outside observer to recognize the difference. Overlapping functions are common; university faculty do both research and teaching, often at the same time, so budget and accounting treatments of the resulting expenses often must be approximate. Some capital expenses may be found in either the operating or capital budgets (this also affects costs) that normally focus only on the operating budget.

Fringe benefits sometimes are budgeted directly to institutions but in other cases are budgeted centrally for all state programs. Such differences can have a major impact on interstate comparisons. Revenues also may be treated differently. Tuition revenues may be kept by the institution or transmitted to the state; this can have a potential impact on institutional budgets. An institution might increase tuition to bring in revenue beyond the formula or budget. The treatment of student fees, as opposed to tuition, varies widely among institutions. Are library fines, for example, retained at the institution or turned over to the state? Also, some activities may be self-supporting and not be in budgets.

If one is counting people, not dollars, other aberrations may occur.

For example, enrollment data are critical in comparisons that typically rely on cost or staffing per student. Institutions may count student enrollments in somewhat differing ways. Although a head count of every student registered appears simple enough, it does not reflect the different workload requirements caused by varying proportions of full-time and part-time students. To equalize work-load requirements, a full-time equivalent student count normally is used, but states and institutions may count such students in varying ways. Summer session enrollments may be counted in different ways or not at all; in addition, potential counting problems arise from using different calendars (quarters, trimesters). How, for example, should graduate teaching assistants, part-time (adjunct) faculty, or faculty with full-time and part-time administrative duties (department chairpersons, associate deans) be counted?

A related data problem is that one year's data may reflect aberrations. A sudden enrollment change, for example, may lead to extraordinarily high or low costs per student. Ideally, one would use data for a series of years rather than for only one year in order to get a clearer picture of institutional comparisons.

Finally, one cannot expect that even with perfect definitions all institutions will report accurately. In the West Virginia study, reporting of medical school expenses and of expenses from federal and other grants and contracts seemed to differ significantly in some cases.

The data comparability problems suggest that in making such comparisons it may be better to use larger than smaller numbers of states or institutions in the sample. Also, a multiple approach to comparisons as used in the West Virginia study appears more desirable than does reliance on a single set of data.

Formulas Versus Budgets Versus Expenditures. In the best of all possible worlds for the researcher, budget formulas would lead directly to budgets, and actual expenditures and revenues would closely reflect the budgets. In the real world all three factors may be tenuously related at best. Often the formulas are not all-inclusive, and it may not be clear what factors are treated outside the formula factors. State budgets may reflect the formulas in many possible ways, depending on the state's fiscal condition, its overall priorities, the politics of institutional relationships in the state, and other factors. These factors are frequently invisible even to the trained researcher's eye. The budget process may use some percentage of the formula, make selective cuts or additions, or not employ the formula at all. Finally, expenditures may be cut or added by a state or institution in many ways during the fiscal year, and the institutions may allocate and shift funds from one formula or budget category to another once the budget is approved. In fact, one advantage of formulas to universities is that they can be used to generate a budget that the university is then free to reallocate as it wishes.

Again, multiple approaches to comparisons are essential as is a knowledge of a state's institutional practices in translating formulas to budgets to actual expenditures. It is helpful to track the process from formula through expenditures.

Formulas. No two states have the same formula for higher education institutions. This fact does not reflect mere contrariness on the part of the states. Rather, formulas usually reflect local histories and situations. Most important, formulas often represent what is rather than what should be. A common approach for developing formulas is to obtain an average of the costs or staffing patterns at the various state institutions. The budget debate then revolves around whether the results are too high or low and how to change them to account for inflation, salary increases, new programs, or other factors.

Formulas frequently are expressed in average unit costs, such as a dollar value per student credit hour taught or per square foot of physical plant maintained. Given the differences possible in salaries and many other factors when comparing across states, it is clear that a cost per lower division credit hour in mathematics will differ considerably across states. Perhaps more significant, since these unit costs simply reflect what actually is happening, there is no certainty that any of the numbers indicate what actually is needed to teach mathematics. The best that can be said (and this may be more than sufficient for analytical purposes) is that such costs provide one representation of the real world, marketplace situation. Given some understanding of the data and applying a formula across all programs, the overall result may be reasonable.

Staffing patterns, as opposed to unit costs, are more readily translatable from place to place. Ratios of teachers to FTE students or custodians per square feet of space are understandable, but must then be translated into dollars; doing so may cause a number of problems.

Formulas frequently appear too simplistic. The question then is, will a more complex formula actually be an improvement? Can a formula become too complex for practical use by political decision makers? For example, the plant maintenance budget could be modeled in a series of increasingly complex ways, as follows:

- Overall cost per square foot
- Cost per square foot for custodian and for all other staff
- Staffing patterns for custodians, skilled tradesmen, heating/cooling plant workers, and groundsmen related to square footage, BTUs, acreage, or similar factors
- One of the above taking into account the age, condition and intensity of use of buildings, type of spaces to be cleaned, type of acreage, and so on.

Varying formulas are used at different levels of the process. In the above examples, a state budget office or legislature might use the first one, a statewide coordinating or governing board the third, and universities the last. In any case, interstate formula comparisons are made difficult by the varying approaches or levels of complexity, and questions always remain about the validity of the formulas.

In universities many factors cannot be or rarely are formula driven. For example, research or public service activities, energy costs or student financial aid are important programmatically and budgetarily but are almost never formula driven. Many important nonpersonnel items, instructional or computer equipment, or telephone bills, for example, may be included in formulas but with little rationale. Finally, formulas that may work in one place will almost certainly not work elsewhere.

Formulas are subject to manipulation, and such manipulations may affect interinstitutional comparisons. In response to a budget formula that substantially rewarded upper-division course enrollments, the physics department at one of the author's institutions simply classified nearly all its courses as upper division, thereby reaping a formula funding bonanza. If an entire institution followed such a practice, interinstitutional comparisons with that school would be misleading.

Fixed Versus Variable Costs. An issue of considerable importance in higher education formulas and budgeting is that of fixed versus variable costs. In its simplest expression, a university needs one president whether it has three thousand or thirty thousand students. The larger school usually would, as a result, have a much lower cost per student. At the other extreme, if the same institutions had the same amount of building square footage per student, their plant maintenance costs per student might be roughly the same.

Formulas may take fixed costs into account in varying ways, or the budgets may do so independently of the formulas. A formula might, for example, provide a fixed number of staff for a function regardless of institutional size, with decreasing increments of staff for larger institutions. The presence or absence of approaches to fixed versus variable costs in formulas and budgets must be evaluated when interinstitutional comparisons are made, particularly when work-load factors are in flux.

Timeliness. The latest available data on formulas for comparison purposes often are several years old. If comparisons are made of unit costs, this can be a serious problem, since the analyst does not know how the costs have changed or if they have. In preparing an annual budget, data even a year or two old seems hopelessly out of date, particularly if inflation is high. Staffing pattern formulas, of course, cause less problems in this regard. The analyst may try to overcome this problem by seeking data directly from the institutions or states rather than using national data but may then have more problems with data comparability.

These are some of the many technical problems that may arise when interinstitutional comparisons are made of budget formulas and data. The analyst may have difficulty knowing that such problems exist without a reasonably detailed understanding of the material. Funding formulas or cost distributions are not directly transferable among states.

Notwithstanding the potential problems, a reasonably careful inter-institutional comparison based on application of appropriate formulas and analyses of actual expenditures and revenues should in many cases prove helpful in making resource allocation decisions. There is no substitute for careful analysis of the needs of a given program based on its specific goals, program mix, size, history, and other factors, but interstate and interinstitutional comparisons can provide an excellent check on the findings in the basic analysis.

Political Problems

While it is important to understand the technical difficulties in comparative analysis, it is also crucial to understand the political problems likely to be encountered.

Political participants, including other colleges and universities, are likely to view an attempt at peer analysis, especially a first-time effort, from their own perspective and then use the analysis for their own purposes. In the case of West Virginia, individuals already opposed to the existence of the Regents readily recognized the most critical aspects of the peer analysis even though these political actors had not in the past been supportive of WVU.

If institutions are to use comparative analysis effectively in budget advocacy, the analysis must be linked to a broader strategy of external relations. When WVU's financial analysis was only an analytical study, it could be ignored. When it received statewide public attention, it was taken more seriously.

Limitations. Attempts to generate comparative analysis encounter certain inherent limitations in a political world. Data always lag behind current events—sometimes much behind. HEGIS data and Advisory Commission on Intergovernmental Relations (ACIR) data (both used with great care in the study reported here) seem very out of date when considering next year's budget proposals. Sometimes there are other not obvious but nonetheless important changes. West Virginia was experiencing a dramatic downturn in its economy, and hence tax capacity, in the period of this analysis, as subsequent ACIR data have revealed. Nevertheless, as low as West Virginia was on tax capacity, it was still lower on tax effort.

Even when an analysis is well done, if it is not favorable or consistent with long-held beliefs, it will be doubted. At WVU the analysis showed the university to be below its peers in every category except one: the library. Both methodological approaches suggested that the library was overfunded compared with other campus activities, even if the analysts pointed out that the collection was smaller than required by standard acquisition formulas and visiting library accreditation panels had commented that the library was underfunded.

The contradictions about the library could be explained in many ways. WVU operates a decentralized library system, with many specialized libraries at various locations, and perhaps this costs more. Also, WVU has used little modern technology in its library operations. Perhaps these two elements combine to make the library a very labor-intensive and hence expensive operation. In any case, the interinstitutional analysis challenged conventional wisdom regarding the WVU library. At least an additional study should have been made, but given the strongly held conventional beliefs, there was no follow-up study.

Changing Budgeting. If interinstitutional analysis cannot change politics and the political world, it can at least change the way budgeting is performed. Suddenly, perhaps for the first time, many key individuals in higher education in West Virginia (the Regents, individuals in the legislature and at other institutions) were examining the fundamental patterns of funding institutions and were, in some cases, suddenly checking with other nearby states to determine how they financed public colleges and universities.

Invoking comparative financial analysis often means that other participants must respond using analysis. Sometimes this has little or no effect on short-term budgetary results, but it is likely to have some long-term impacts.

In the two years that have ensued since the Benedum panel completed its study, the pressure for and support of peer institution comparisons have grown. Evidence of this can be found in the discussions of budgetary problems in higher education in the state legislature as well as in the budget preparations presented by the state's universities and colleges. In the case of West Virginia University, comparisons of peer institutions in terms of formula applications and compensation levels for faculty and staff have been used before the Board of Regents in its last two budgetary presentations. There has been gradual but discernible progress toward acceptance of peer institution data for all colleges and universities within the system. Related to this development has been the greater use of comparative data for peer institutions that comprise the Southern Regional Education Board of which West Virginia is a member.

In contrast, comparisons made for many years prior to the Benedum study and the financial analysis that was included focused heavily on in-state comparisons among highly dissimilar institutions. It is clear that these simplistic comparisons have begun to decline in favor of real peer data and analytical approaches.

Another real gain made is the increased attention now being devoted to differentiating the missions of the various colleges and universities in

West Virginia. The use of peer comparisons and at least the beginning of an understanding of how higher education formulas work and are applied elsewhere have helped develop deeper understanding. It is also evident that continuous repetition of the importance of mission and reinforcement of peer comparison are keys to creating greater financial support for higher education in general and for West Virginia University in particular.

The West Virginia University experience illustrates another value of peer comparisons and use of formulas: These studies can provide a basis on which consensus can be built on what the University's legitimate aspiration level should be. The two major reference frameworks used in the study—the eighteen-peer institutions and the four comparative institutions in neighboring states—provided useful reference points for setting aspiration levels.

They also served a second important function: as a means of cross-checking reference groups. Many public policymakers are highly suspicious of how data are packaged and how information can be manipulated to the advantage of an academic institution or an entire system of public higher education that is competing for support with other major governmental program areas. The dual methodology employed reduces the basis for such criticism and offers a means of verification that a single methodology would not provide.

Another realization that has occurred since the Benedum study is that all higher education institutions within the state of West Virginia will benefit from the increased support that can result if peer comparisons were used. The real value here is that hostilities among widely disparate institutions in the state may diminish somewhat as it becomes apparent that a united front can benefit all institutions. Coupled with the fact that hard data can be developed in support of efforts to increase the total funding of higher education, this systemwide benefit is becoming more important.

Implications

We have reported an actual case study where an institution began systematic interinstitutional analysis for the first time and used that information in its budgetary advocacy. In some ways WVU is close to a worst-case scenario in that it was seriously underfunded. Yet the immediate results in terms of real dollars were minimal.

The WVU story suggests that a one-time, "quick and dirty" analysis is probably not all that helpful for short-term budget advocacy. Although outside experts can assist an institution in starting comparative analysis and provide some legitimacy for the approach, both technical and political issues suggest that the biggest benefit is in gaining long-range perspective.

Change comes slowly in a state that moves from a highly subjective basis for securing and allocating higher education funds to a more factually based approach. Opinions of key decision makers are slow to change. Measuring the impact of specific analytical approaches to higher education funding is also slow. The results simply do not appear within a year or two. It is likely that the greatest impact of the approaches reviewed here will be on long-range attitudes and the ways in which participants deal with budgeting and resource allocation in the coming years.

References

Academy for Educational Development. *Revitalization and Renewal: The Report of the Benedum Study Project at West Virginia University.* New York: Academy for Educational Development, 1984.

Advisory Commission of Intergovernmental Relations. *1981 Tax Capacity of the Fifty States.* Washington, D.C.: Advisory Commission on Intergovernmental Relations, 1983.

Lane, F. S., and Lawrence, J. S. *State Funding of West Virginia University: A Comparative Analysis of West Virginia University and Peer Institutions.* Morgantown: Office of the Vice President for Administration and Finance, West Virginia University, 1984.

WVU Funding. *Intelligencer,* November 20, 1984, (editorial).

Frederick S. Lane is professor of public administration at Bernard M. Baruch College, City University of New York.

James S. Lawrence is vice-president for finance and management, City College, City University of New York.

Herman Mertins, Jr., is vice-president for administration and finance and professor of public administration, West Virginia University.

Getting the most from interinstitutional comparisons requires some effort. Careful planning will increase the chances of success. Long-run effects may have the greatest impact.

Effective Interinstitutional Comparisons

Paul T. Brinkman

Three themes are predominate in the foregoing chapters: First, successful use of interinstitutional comparisons does not just happen. It requires effort, sometimes considerable effort, to carry through what often is a complex process. Second, careful planning can help ensure success. Third, comparative analyses can have important long-run effects even when they fail to produce the desired immediate results.

The proliferation of secondary data sources documented by Christal and Wittstruck has made the current acquisition of data easier than it was a decade ago. Efforts at standardization and the familiarity gained through the continued use of major data resources such as HEGIS have smoothed out some of the bumps that are a regular part of comparative analyses among institutions. But every such analysis has the potential to raise or uncover new problems associated with the comparability of particular data items. As a result, the conscientious institutional researcher has little choice but to remain vigilant, to assume as little as possible about the validity of the data, and to think through the various possibilities, including record keeping and reporting problems, that might explain apparent differences in the behavior of institutions.

An alternative to using secondary data bases for comparative data is to establish a data exchange network. In his insightful commentary on this

P. T. Brinkman (ed.). *Conducting Interinstitutional Comparisons.*
New Directions for Institutional Research, no. 53. San Francisco: Jossey-Bass, Spring 1987.

option, Dunn shows why a full-fledged, formal arrangement is not for everyone. Formal data sharing is hard work, and the requirements for ongoing planning and management are substantial; almost anyone would think twice about undertaking such a venture. But the number of such arrangements seems to be growing. Apparently the hard work pays off. Many informal data-sharing arrangements exist as well. Requiring only a modest amount of effort, they offer a viable means of augmenting nationally available data. The trade-off is that they typically lack the assurance of data compatibility, the essential bottom line of formal arrangements.

Finding good comparative data is only part of the problem. The data need to be aggregated, related, and structured so that they can be meaningfully interpreted. This occurs most often and most readily in the context of data on groups of institutions, as opposed to one-to-one comparisons. Brinkman and Teeter set out a typology for the various kinds of groups that are being used. Perhaps the critical element of their discussion, although they do not use this language, is that comparison group membership is, in part, psychological. We use our mental powers to create group membership and give it meaning. What is the implication? The expectations and understandings that go into or that structure a comparison are crucial. Virtually everything important to the comparison depends on planning and forethought. In other words, one should have answers to such questions as: Are the institutions expected to behave in the same way or differently? On what grounds? What is the theoretical framework of the comparison? An example of such a framework would be microeconomic theory, which suggests that smaller institutions in a comparison group might be expected to have higher unit costs just because they are smaller. In a given situation this may be false, but at least it gives meaning to data.

Whiteley and Stage take the planning premise a step further. They wish to include it in the collective consciousness of the whole enterprise by bringing comparative analysis and comparison groups fully into the institution's formal planning process. They argue that if comparisons occur elsewhere, they are likely to cause trouble. Unplanned and uncoordinated comparisons may send conflicting messages to internal and external constituencies, and their ad hoc use can as easily be disruptive as helpful.

Whiteley and Stage also argue that a philosophy of comparison is needed as a foundation for comparative activities. There are indeed interesting philosophical questions to be asked. For example, consider how one might justify the use of comparative data as the basis for decisions regarding an appropriate level of funding for a given educational program. Because the educational production function remains somewhat mysterious (our knowledge of the circumstances and conditions that govern learning are incomplete), one can make the case that an absolute framework against which to measure alternative funding levels simply does not exist. In its absence a relative framework in which one looks to what is happening elsewhere is appealing. It would seem to make at least as much as sense as a simple retrospective of previous funding levels. Yet, adopting a relative framework appears to entail the surrender of sovereignty, in a manner of speaking. This might make sense if decision makers in other institutions or state legislators could be counted on to have superior knowledge.

Perhaps some of the desired theoretical underpinnings could be derived from comparative organizational research as practiced in a number of disciplines such as sociology and political science. Nagging questions about values and purposes are likely to remain, however, especially about comparative analyses that are meant to undergird decision making rather than enhance understanding.

One of the major developments over the past decade is the increased use of interinstitutional comparisons at the state level. What was once occasional has now become commonplace, and the number of states so involved continues to grow. For institutions in the public sector this is serious business, since more often than not some aspect of financial support, typically for either faculty salaries or overall funding, will depend in part on the outcomes of these comparative analyses. Thus, the need for comparative approaches that are both technically and philosophically sound is anything but academic.

In discussing comparative analysis from the state, as well as the system, perspective, Marilyn McCoy stresses a theme that also appears in several other chapters. For all the importance of technical issues, there is no substitute for careful attention to the overall process of using comparative analysis. That process is especially complex when its locus is a system or state office. Among the tasks that must be attended to are setting an agenda, ensuring that institutions have adequate participation, disseminating information widely, and attending to the political context in which the use of the analysis will ultimately be decided. The author also makes the point that system- and state-level staff should endeavor to build institutional profiles as the basis for comparative analysis. Isolated bits of comparative data taken out of context have as much potential for doing harm as for providing insights helpful in decision making.

The concluding themes of Chapter Six by Lane, Lawrence, and Mertins are particularly important for assessing the effectiveness of interinstitutional comparisons. As the authors indicate, the comparison they undertook did not yield the intended benefit of an increased level of funding for West Virginia University. Yet, they argue that the comparative analysis had a significant impact in two ways: It changed the ground rules for the funding process. The parties involved now look outward to other states as well as inward as they endeavor to find the appropriate level of funding within the state's budgetary constraints. The authors interpret this as a gain in rationality that, given the particulars of the situation, may well result in long-term benefits to the state's higher education institutions.

The authors' comparative analysis has also sharpened the debate about the mission of West Virginia University. Mission statements are often full of rhetoric and not very concrete. Comparative analysis can help institutions delineate their own identity in relatively concrete terms. In this regard, interinstitutional comparisons can be a helpful antidote to state coordination efforts that, unwittingly or otherwise, can blur useful distinctions among institutions within a state. Of course, more clearly defining an institution's mission can have other unlooked-for results, so there is good reason to think through the potential impact of comparative analysis.

Below are two lists of articles and books on interinstitutional comparisons in higher education. The first list contains publications that address procedural matters concerned primarily with the selection of comparison institutions. The publications of the second list demonstrate or discuss how interinstitutional comparisons can and have been used in higher education. The examples they provide are only illustrations, because most comparative work of this type is not published.

One publication that should be mentioned is Peterson's *Benefiting from Interinstitutional Research* (1976), an earlier volume of this *New Directions for Institutional Research* series. A few chapters, such as those on national data bases or about the then-nascent electronic data-sharing networks, have lost some relevance over the intervening decade, but the volume as a whole still contains much that is useful to anyone involved in interinstitutional comparisons. This volume and the current one can be considered companion volumes. Together they provide extensive coverage of the problems, opportunities, and responsibilities that are part of comparative institutional analysis in higher education.

Methodology for Selecting Comparison Groups

Astin, A. W. "An Empirical Characterization of Higher Education Institutions." In K. A. Feldman (ed.), *College and Student*. New York: Pergamon, 1972.

Baldridge, J. V., Curtis, D. V., Ecker, G., and Riley, G. L. "Diversity in Higher Education: Professonal Autonomy." *Journal of Higher Education*, 1977, *48*, 367-388.

Blau, P. M. "A Formal Theory of Differentiation in Organizations." *American Sociological Review*, 1970, *35*, 201-218.

Carnegie Commission on Higher Education. *A Classification of Institutions of Higher Education*. Berkeley, Calif.: Carnegie Commission on Higher Education, 1976.

Carter, D. A., and Pollis, R. "Budgeting and Accounting: There's No Place Like Alaska—or Nevada." *College and University Business*, 1974, *56*, 6-7.

Cleaver, G. S. "Analysis to Determine a Ranking in Similarity for Institutions in Higher Education." Paper presented at the Annual Conference of the Society for College and University Planning, Omaha, Nebraska, July 12-15, 1981.

Creswell, J. W., Roskins, R. W., and Henry, T. C. "A Typology of Multicampus Systems." *Journal of Higher Education*, 1985, *56* (1), 26-37.

Elsass, J. E., and Lingenfelter, P. E. *An Identification of College and University Peer Groups*. Springfield: Illinois Board of Education, 1980.

Moden, G. C., and Schrader, M. "Benchmark Analysis Among Public Institutions." Paper presented at the Twenty-Second Annual Forum of the Association for Institutional Research, Denver, Colorado, May 16-19, 1982.

Pace, C. R. *The Demise of Diversity: A Comparative Profile of Eight Types of Institutions*. Berkeley: The Carnegie Foundation for the Advancement of Teaching, 1974.

Rawson, J., Hoyt, D., and Teeter, D. "Identifying 'Comparable' Institutions." *Research in Higher Education*, 1983, *18* (3), 299-310.

Rowse, G. L., and Wing, P. "Assessing Competitive Structures in Higher Education." *Journal of Higher Education*, 1982, *53*, 656-686.

Smart, J. C. "Diversity of Academic Organizations." *Journal of Higher Education*, 1978, *49*, 403-419.

Smart, J. C., Elton, C. F., and Martin, R. O. "Qualitative and Conventional Indices of Benchmark Institutions." Paper presented at the Twentieth Annual Forum of the Association for Institutional Research, Atlanta, Georgia, April 29, 1980.

Smith, P., and Henderson, C. *A Financial Taxonomy of Institutions of Higher Education*. Washington, D.C.: American Council on Education, 1976.

Stadtman, V. A. *Academic Adaptations*. San Francisco: Jossey-Bass, 1980.

Teeter, D. J. "The Politics of Comparing Data with Other Institutions." In J. W. Firnberg and W. F. Lasher (eds.), *The Politics and Pragmatics of Institutional Research*. New Directions for Institutional Research, no. 38. San Francisco: Jossey-Bass, 1983.

Terenzini, P. T., Hartmark, L., Lorang, W. G., Jr., and Shirley, R. C. "A Conceptual and Methodological Approach to the Identification of Peer Institutions." *Research in Higher Education*, 1980, *12*, 347-364.

Using Interinstitutional Comparisons

Board of Educational Finance. *Higher Education in New Mexico: A Study of Average Faculty Salaries and Compensation for New Mexico's Universities and Their Comparison-Group Institutions*. Sante Fe, N.M.: Board of Educational Finance and the Legislative Finance Committee in cooperation with the six universities, November, 1985.

Brush, S. G., Menzer, R. E., and Beale, R. S. *Research in Major State Universities: Some Quantitative Measures*. College Park: University of Maryland, 1976.

Dickmeyer, N., and Cirino, A. M. *Comparative Financial Statistics for Public Community and Junior Colleges: 1983-1984*. Washington, D.C.: National Association of College and University Business Officers, 1985.

Dunham, P. C., and Carter, D. *A Comparative Analysis of Expenditures and Support of Public Higher Education in Maine and Selected Comparable and Noncomparable States*. Bangor: Office of Financial Planning, University of Maine, 1975.

Hample, S. R., and Woienski, N. *Faculty Salary Comparisons for MSU, UM, and Peer Institutions, 1982-1983*. Bozeman: Office of Institutional Researchh, Montana State University, 1983.

Hyatt, J. A. "Using National Financial Data for Comparative Analysis." In C. Francis (ed.), *Successful Responses to Financial Difficulty*. New Directions for Higher Education, no. 38. San Francisco: Jossey-Bass, 1982.

Hyatt, J. A., and Thompson, R. K. "State and Institutional Comparative Analyses Using HEGIS Finance Data: A Review." *Business Officer*, 1980, *13*, 20-24.

Kansas Board of Regents. *Relative Funding of the Regents Universities: Fiscal Year 1983.* Topeka: Kansas Board of Regents, 1984.

Lingenfelter, P. E. "The Uses and Abuses of Interstate Comparisons of Higher Education Funding." *Business Officer,* 1983, *17* (3), 14–16.

Minter, J., Nelson, C. A., and Robinson, D. D. *Ratio Analysis in Higher Education: A Guide to Assessing the Institution's Financial Condition.* New York: Peat, Marwick, Mitchell, 1980.

Nebraska Coordinating Commission for Postsecondary Education. *A Study of the Appropriate Tuition Levels for Nebraska Public Postsecondary Institutions.* Lincoln: Nebraska Coordinating Commission for Postsecondary Education, 1984.

Peterson, M. W. (ed.). *Benefiting from Interinstitutional Research.* New Directions for Institutional Research, no. 12. San Francisco: Jossey-Bass, 1976.

State Board for Higher Education. *Faculty Salaries, Rank, and Tenure at Maryland Public Universities and Four-Year Colleges Compared to Designated Peers: Academic Years 1976-1977 to 1981-1982.* Annapolis, Md.: State Board for Higher Education, July 1982.

Paul T. Brinkman is senior associate at the National Center for Higher Education Management Systems, Boulder, Colorado, where he specializes in comparative data issues and higher education finance.

Index

112